THE SCREAM THAT SHOCKS THE SCREEN WITH
300,000 VOLTS OF
HORROR!
INHUMAN!
INVINCIBLE!
INESCAPABLE!
Indestructible
MAN
starring
LON CHANEY
with
MARIAN CARR
Casey Adams • Ross Elliot
PRODUCED AND DIRECTED BY
JACK POLLEXFEN
SCREENPLAY BY
VY RUSSELL AND SUE BRADFORD

Indestructible Man
© 2014 Tom Weaver. All Rights Reserved.

No part of this book may be reproduced in any form or by any means, electronic, mechanical, digital, photocopying or recording, except for the inclusion in a review, without permission in writing from the publisher.

Published in the USA by:
BearManor Media
P. O. Box 71426
Albany, GA 31708
www.bearmanormedia.com

ISBN 978-1-59393-701-0

Printed in the United States of America.
Book design by Robbie Adkins, www.adkinsconsult.com
Cover design by Kerry Gammill; back cover art by Marty Baumann; chapter title graphics by Kez Wilson.

TABLE OF CONTENTS

Introduction by Fred Olen Ray 1

Indestructible Man 3

Indefatigable Man: Jack Pollexfen 8

Unintelligible Man: Aubrey Wisberg 12

The Making of *Indestructible Man* 14

Indispensable Man by Burl Lampert 29

Notes on the Script 33

The Script 37

Inharmonious Man by David Schecter 129

Indisputable Fun Facts 141

Interview with Casey Adams 157

Indestructible Man: **The Release** by Dr. Robert J. Kiss 159

The Man from Planet X Goes Looney Tunes 161

Recommended Additional Viewing .163

Indestructible **Inspiration** 166

Press Book 169

Thank You!: Ron Adams, John Antosiewicz, Casey Adams, Ellen Bailey, Marty "The Butcher" Baumann, Michael F. Blake, Sue Bradford, Ewing Brown, John "Squeamy" Brunas, Mike Brunas, Bob Burns, Robert Clarke, Joe Dante, Bradford Dillman, Ross Elliott, Kerry Gammill, Robert Guffey, Paul Haight, Richard Heft, Dr. Robert J. Kiss, Burl Lampert, Dan Lewis, Scott MacQueen, Boyd Magers, Mark Martucci, Jack Pollexfen, Lee Pollexfen, Fred Olen Ray, Gary Rhodes, Alan Rode, Vy Russell, William Schallert, David Schecter, Rich Scrivani, Robert Shayne, Laura Wagner, Kez Wilson, Tom Woodruff Jr.

(Allied Artists, 1956)
Cast and Credits

C.G.K. Productions; Produced & Directed by Jack Pollexfen; Original Screenplay: Vy Russell & Sue Bradford; Photography: John Russell Jr.; Editor: Fred Feitshans Jr.; Art Director: Ted Holsopple; Production Manager: Chris Beute; **Uncredited**: Music Director: Albert Glasser; 70 minutes

Lon Chaney (*Charles "Butcher" Benton*), Casey Adams (*Police Lt. Dick Chasen*), Marian Carr (*Eva Martin*), Ross Elliott (*Paul Lowe*), Stuart Randall (*Police Capt. John I. Lauder*), Ken Terrell (*Joe Marcelli*), Robert Foulk (*Harry—Bartender*), Marjorie Stapp (*Girl in Car*), Rita Green (*Carney's Girl*), Robert Shayne (*Dr. Bradshaw*), Roy Engel (*Police Sergeant*), Peggy Maley (*Francine*), Madge Cleveland (*Screaming Woman Attendant*); **Uncredited**: Marvin Press (*Squeamy Ellis*), Joe Flynn (*Bradshaw's Assistant*), Eddie Marr (*Carney*), Dorothy Ford (*Stripper*); **In stock footage from *He Walked by Night* (1948)**: Harlan Warde (*Police Operator*), Ann Doran (*Police Dispatcher*).

INTRODUCTORY MAN

Fred Olen Ray

I have always loved *Indestructible Man*. I've watched it probably a dozen times. I even started a remake of it and shot some scenes with actor Aldo Ray in the Lon Chaney role (I'll let you figure that part out). I'm not sure why I love it so much, but I've got a few educated hunches of my own...and a few offered up by my shrink.

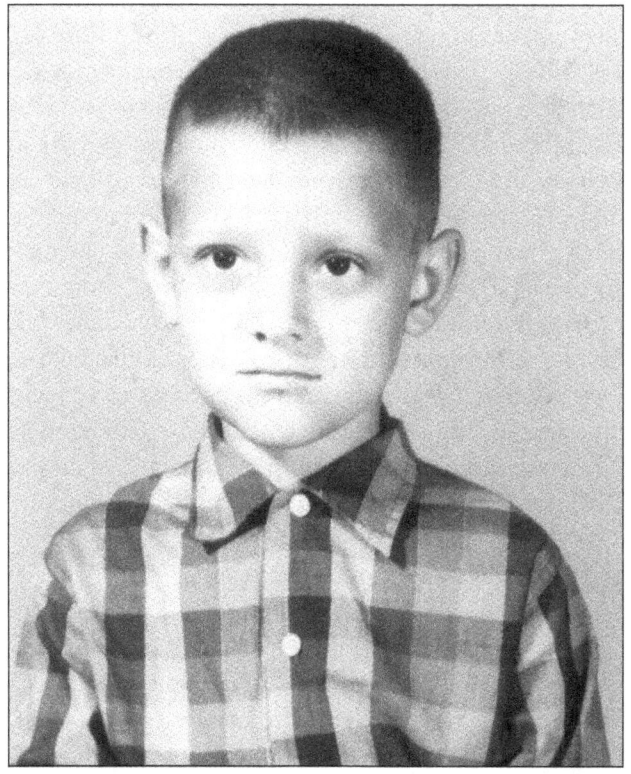

Fred Olen Ray at just the right age for the schlock shocks of *The Astounding She-Monster, Giant from the Unknown* and *Indestructible Man*.

There are a lot of films from my youth that I hold dear regardless of what time has shown me of them. Most likely it has to do with my initial childhood memory of seeing them as a wound-up kid glued to the flickering cathode ray TV in my Aunt Garnet's house in West Virginia 40-odd years ago. Cinematic gems like *The Astounding She-Monster* and *Giant from the Unknown* and, yes, I'll admit it, *The Beast with a Million Eyes*. If I had first watched these as an adult, I probably wouldn't feel the same way about them, but for better or worse (I'll say "better") I flat-out love these old clunkers.

A somewhat more recent photo of writer-producer-director Ray (right), seen here with Christian Slater, star of his 2012 film *Hatfields and McCoys: Bad Blood*.

Lon Chaney was my favorite actor when I was a kid; still is. I would eagerly seek out and watch anything he was in, but due to his continually sliding career, most of what I could lay eyes on were usually small guest appearances and pointless cameos. Who could forget the throwaway role in *The Big Chase* (1954)...he doesn't even have a line of dialogue in the film.

The idea that he was actually the uncontested star of *Indestructible Man* and portrayed a "sort of" monster role was enough to send me scrambling. The fact that it aped Universal's *Man Made Monster* (1941) to a certain degree didn't seem like a bad idea at the time either.

I also appreciated the *Dragnet* style of gritty realism the film embraced. The producer's decision to utilize authentic urban locations afforded the viewer a glimpse at 1950s Los Angeles, reminiscent of the unvarnished opening montage sequence in Gordon Parks' *Shaft* (1971).

The straight-ahead storyline moves briskly, dropping the audience right into the middle of the action without any lengthy rigmarole leading up to the Butcher's upcoming execution. And Lon is afforded the kind of coveted on-screen time and importance that horror fans had been hungering for...at least this fan, anyway. It was, finally, a real Lon Chaney movie.

I don't necessarily agree, however, as some others have implied, that Chaney's dialogue was bare-bones because of his drinking issues. Lon appeared in movies and on television in a variety of productions such as Martin and Lewis' *Pardners* (1956) and the poignant *Telephone Time* episode "The Golden Junkman" around that same time, turning in one of his finer late career performances. I think the lack of dialogue in *Indestructible Man* was vitally important and played an essential role in elevating Chaney's brutish criminal "Butcher" Benton to a bona fide "monster" character without straining the film's already meager budget.

I also embraced the "police procedural" tone of the movie; it gave the film a documentary flavor; like it might really have happened...but, who am I kidding? I just love anything with Lon Chaney in it and this film gave the fading star the titular role I had been waiting for. That it happened to be a real Lon Chaney "monster" flick made it all the sweeter.

So to say I am delighted to be a part of this book should go *without* saying! I plan on reading (and re-reading) every word of it!

By Tom Weaver

high´ con´cept
n.
a simple and often striking idea or premise, as for a story or film, that lends itself to easy promotion.

The descriptor "high concept" appears to have been coined in the 1980s—but decades in advance, the screenwriting team of Jack Pollexfen and Aubrey Wisberg devised a long series of B-pictures that fell under that heading, with Pollexfen and Wisberg often placing famous real-life or fictional characters at the hub of their plots. Had we been around to sit in on their pitch meetings, we might have heard hard-sell spiels like:

Treasure of Monte Cristo (1949): "A modern-day descendant of the Count of Monte Cristo battles crooks who are after his ancestor's treasure!"

The Desert Hawk (1950): "Two thousand years ago, a hero called the Desert Hawk and his pals Sinbad and Aladdin prevent the wedding of the Princess Shaharazade!"

At Sword's Point (1952): "She's in a fix so the queen of France sends for the Three Musketeers. They're now too old to fight so *they* send their sons—and a *daughter*!"

Captain John Smith and Pocahontas (1953): "This is not your grandmother's John Smith and Pocahontas: We've sexed it up!"

And on and on courtesy of a daughter of Treasure Island and the slave girl of Captain Kidd and a *Lady* in the Iron Mask and more. They were B-movies through and through, the concepts as high as the budgets were low. All the characters were caricatures, and any resemblance to real persons, living or dead, was purely out of the question.

Pollexfen and Wisberg split in the mid-1950s but both subsequently stayed true to their schlock roots. Among other credits, Wisberg wrote the dire *Mission Mars* (1968) with Darren McGavin and Nick Adams, infamous for its scenes of Earth astronauts exploring the Red Planet wearing motorcycle helmets, and wrote and produced *Hercules in New York* (1969) with Arnold Stang and Arnold Schwarzenegger. Pollexfen's additions to his résumé, *Daughter of Dr. Jekyll* (1957) and *Monstrosity* (1963), were nearly as dreary. *Monstrosity*, in fact, is quite the disasterpiece.

But before Pollexfen foisted those two desultory titles on audiences, he did hit the bad-film bull's-eye one time: He combined a familiar sci-fi premise with an equally familiar gangster storyline, gave it rock-bottom production values and somehow wound up with a junk-movie gem: *Indestructible Man*. It's a monster movie without a monster, just Lon Chaney as a convicted killer who trudges to the Hereafter (the San Quentin gas chamber) but is later reanimated, ambling around L.A. in a knee-length fur-collar overcoat looking to settle some old scores. But what Monster Kid has ever griped? You've got Chaney, his sideburns and barberphobic mop of hair, his onion-peeling-quivery-eyes closeups and over-the-top rampages, the *Dragnet*-

"Some low-budget 'cult' films are easy to define. *Plan 9* is laughable. *Invaders from Mars* is a miracle. But *Indestructible Man* is…indestructible. Just why is a little hard to explain."—Ronald L. Smith, *VideoScope* magazine

style presentation, seedy downtown L.A. atmosphere and Albert Glasser's bombastic score—in other words, more than enough pleasing elements that most of us have seen it a dozen times or more (probably more) since we first lapped it up on some TV *Creature Features* program of our childhood.

To greatly paraphrase Benjamin Franklin, in this world nothing can be said to be certain except death and taxes and, if you're a Lon Chaney Jr. fan, you love *Indestructible Man*.

Synopsis

In Los Angeles' Hall of Justice, behind the frosted glass door of the Detective Division, Police Lt. Dick Chasen is "dictating the wrap-up on the 'Butcher' Benton package." Throughout the movie we hear this "wrap-up" as narration, Sgt. Friday-*Dragnet* style.

In flashbacks, we see Benton—part of the gang that stole an armored car and the $600,000 in it—awaiting execution on San Quentin's Death Row. He's visited by his lawyer Paul Lowe; Lowe, mastermind of the armored car heist, now wants to know where Benton hid the money. Benton's murder trial was a whistle stop on his fast-track trip to the death house; Lowe purposely botched his defense to insure his execution. Benton knows this, and swears to get revenge on Lowe and their criminal cohorts Squeamy Ellis and Joe Marcelli. Lowe snickers, "You thick-headed ape… you're gonna *die* tomorrow." Benton makes a rueful "oh yeah…I forgot…" face, then reiterates his threat.

With Benton's 5 p.m. gas chamber execution looming, Lt. Chasen is taken off the case by his superior Capt. Lauder, but says he'll continue working on it on his own time. He visits the burlesque house where Benton's gal pal Eva Martin performs, to press her once more about Benton and the whereabouts of the stolen money. Despite her occupation, she's a wholesome small-town girl and was never romantically involved

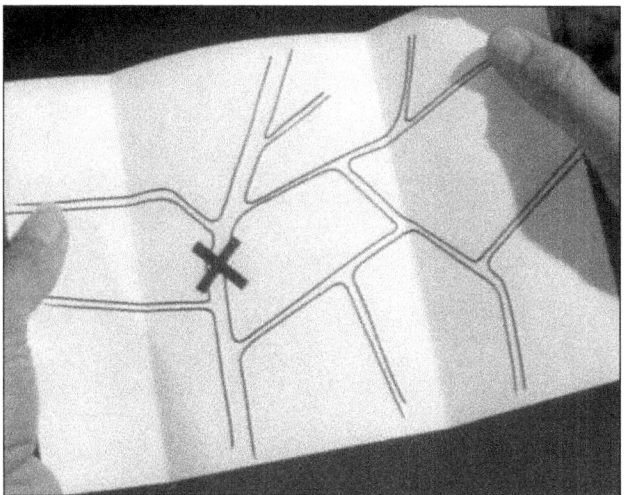

If you were handed this piece of paper, you'd instantly recognize it as a map of part of your city's sewer system and you could make a beeline to the spot marked by the X, yes?

with the Butcher. Eva's next visitor is Lowe, entering her dressing room as a radio newscaster is announcing that, a few moments ago, Benton "paid for his crimes against society in the gas chamber at San Quentin." Depressed by the news, Eva produces a sealed letter envelope which Benton told her to open in the event of his death. When Eva is called away, Lowe opens it and finds a map of the city's sewer system with an X indicating the spot where the $600,000 is hidden.

In San Francisco, biochemist Dr. Bradshaw and his assistant get hold of Benton's body and, as part of their search for a cancer cure, subject it to a 287,000-volt charge. The zap has the wholly unexpected effect of bringing Benton back to life: His vocal cords are burned out by the voltage but, on the plus side, he's now terrifically strong and, says Bradshaw, "his tissue must be nearly a solid mass of cells." Or, as the narrator of the movie's theatrical trailer puts it, Bradshaw's

Little Charlie Benton must have played hooky from school the day it was taught that, if you make the police come get you, they're bringin' an ass-kickin' *with* 'em. Here in *Indestructible Man*'s final reel, Johnny Law enters the L.A. sewers in search of the Butcher.

Below the streets of L.A., no place you'd want to be, Benton (Chaney) finds himself on the wrong end of a flame thrower—no place *anybody*'d want to be! This scene takes place in the sewer in the movie but it was actually shot in a cave (see background wall).

experiment "made his skin as tough as armor plate, and released every killer's instinct stored up in his demented mind!" Benton simultaneously strangles Bradshaw and the assistant and, remembering his promise to kill Lowe, Squeamy and Joe, sets out for L.A.

Heading downstate on foot, he comes across a carnival man named Carney and a girl, stranded because their sporty 1954 Oldsmobile convertible has a flat. Benton lifts the car's front end so that Carney can change the tire, then goes from human jack to carjack, killing Carney and driving away. At a roadblock, the bullets of two highway patrolmen have no effect on him. We later see him putting on a coat he found in Carney's car; Benton was bigger than Carney and yet the coat is a bit big on *him*. Even in black-and-white it's pretty obvious that Carney's car is white but the police are told to watch for his green coupe.

Arriving at the burlesque house, Benton confronts a shocked Eva, showing her bullet holes in his shirt and harmlessly jabbing his own hand with scissors to make her aware of his new'n'improved condition. When Benton realizes that Lowe stole the sewer map, he rushes out with murder in his eye. First he meets up with Joe in the Bunker Hill area, chasing him into an alley and fighting with him amidst garbage cans and clothes on a clothesline. Benton effortlessly gets the upper hand, lifts Joe overhead and throws him (well, a dummy) down a long steep staircase. Now that he's scrambled *that* yegg, he goes to Lowe's fifth-floor Bradbury Building office but instead encounters Squeamy there. Squeamy fires about ten shots from his six-shootin' .38 before Benton picks him up and drops him over an ornate iron railing, down into the building's Victorian court. Eva arrives at the crime scene and hears that the murdered man was named Squeamy, prompting her to ask, "You mean Squeamy *Ellis*?" Apparently Eva knows more than one Squeamy. In a car parked near a sump, a woman describes to police how Benton lifted her boyfriend Jimmy overhead and broke his back ("I heard it *snap!*").

Lowe knows he's next on Benton's hit parade and, breaking under the considerable strain of having a bulletproof maniac on his trail, *wants* the cops to lock him away, out of reach of the Butcher. In exchange for this protection, he must confess to his part in the armored car hold-up. When the cops learn that the stolen loot is stashed in the L.A. sewer system, they assume that's also where Benton is hiding, and soon the lawmen are swarming through those wet catacombs. The sound of Benton ripping open the cash-filled strongbox brings the minions of the law a-running: Without waiting for Benton to make a wrong move, they begin dispensing street justice out of gun barrels, out of a bazooka and even a flame thrower.

His face badly burned, his clothes tattered, Benton exits the sewer through a manhole and finds himself amidst the electrical jungle of a power station. To end his own existence, he sets some machinery into dangerous motion and waits atop a metal structure for the electrical charges and explosion which prove him quite destructible.

In his car on a nighttime date with Eva at a hamburger drive-in, Chasen tells the delighted girl that he's making her his wife.

INDEFATIGABLE MAN: Jack Pollexfen

By Tom Weaver

Born in San Diego, California, on June 10, 1908, Jack Dore Pollexfen was raised in Mill Valley. Fascinated with newspaper work, he began in that business as a copyboy, then moved up to reporter and feature writer on other dailies. Magazine writing assignments led to scriptwriting chores at MGM, Universal and Columbia. (See page 150 for a fuller description of Pollexfen's early years.)

Pollexfen entered into a prolific period once he teamed with London-born screenwriter Wisberg. Their first collaboration to reach the screen was 1949's *Treasure of Monte Cristo*, with Pollexfen and Wisberg providing the screenplay, serving as associate producers and, according to an April 1949 *Variety* item, even accompanying producer Leonard S. Picker and cameraman Benjamin Kline to San Francisco to scout locations. Frisco's sights provided a neat backdrop for this cut-above low-budgeter, shot in May and June 1949 with future mister and missus Glenn Langan and Adele Jergens in the leads. This being a Robert L. Lippert production, the supporting cast naturally included Margia Dean and Sid Melton.

The following year, 1950, Pollexfen and Wisberg wrote the sci-fi script *The Man from Planet X* with the intention of selling it. But they then realized that it could be made on a very low budget and decided to take the production plunge. On November 21, 1950, just days after they wrapped up their writing chores on RKO's *At Sword's Point*, their new independent company Mid-Century Productions was established on the Hal Roach lot. Roach was also where they shot *Planet X*, an eerie tale of a diminutive, bubble-helmeted alien, the advance scout for an invasion fleet, prowling the eerie moors of an island off the coast of Scotland. The producers and director Edgar G. Ulmer cut every corner except in the imagination department, employing parts of castle sets left over from the epic *Joan of Arc* (1948) and using fog to help disguise the fact that the exteriors were actually shot on a small Roach soundstage.

"Jack and his partner Aubrey Wisberg started me off in the business of doing science fiction films," says actor William Schallert, 28 in 1950 when he played *Planet X*'s avaricious Dr. Mears. He additionally told me:

> They were taking a gamble on me—I didn't have much of a track record at the time, except in the small theater in Hollywood. But they cast me in a key role and it worked and I got very good billing. So I was always very grateful to them for that.
>
> But in addition, they backed up their initial belief in me by casting me in I don't remember exactly how many, I haven't counted 'em up, but there's probably five or six pictures that I did for them after that. Jack Pollexfen once told me how they went about casting me: "We would cast as many parts in the picture as we could, and there would always be one left over that was a key part, but we couldn't figure out who to cast in it. And I would always say to Aubrey, 'Well, we gotta cast Bill Schallert. He can do *any*thing.'" And he somehow also managed to convey that belief to Albert Zugsmith, who then cast me in a lot of *his* pictures on the same premise, that I could do *any*thing; that provided me with a fair amount of work over the years. For a character actor to be told ["He can do *any*thing"] early on by somebody who was in a position to hire him, was a real boost to my morale and to my belief in myself. I owe Jack a *lot* for that.

The camera gets in close on Robert Clarke and Margaret Field, stars of Wisberg-Pollexfen's first production *The Man from Planet X.*

"Jack Pollexfen was a workaholic before the word was coined," *Planet X* star Robert Clarke recalled for me. "Aubrey was big on talking—you never had to encourage him. But, as I observed it, it was more talk than elbow grease. Jack was the one to always take the heavier end of things." In addition to co-producing these movies, Pollexfen was usually also their uncredited production manager. Pollexfen wrote me, "I was on the set from well before the day's shooting started, to some time that night when we looked at the previous day's rushes."

"Jack had a very ingratiating personality," Schallert continued. "Aubrey was very British, Jack was very American. He was very gentle and had a really nice sense of humor. He was always there on the set, *very* devoted to the projects."

Los Angeles exhibitor Sherrill Corwin thought *Planet X* had good box office potential, bought the movie outright and got it released through United Artists. The 1950s' first man-from-space movie to go into distribution, it was a moneymaker—as were most of the other SF titles at that moment in time, from the outer space-set *Destination Moon* and *Rocketship X-M* (both 1950) to the Earthbound *The Thing from Another World* (1951). According to the *Variety* article "Studios Rocketing Out of World Via Scientifiction Pix" (April 18, 1951), *The Thing*'s success had the majority of movie companies

> going all out in search of similar science fiction and pseudo-scientific subjects. ...[The studios'] story departments have their eyes open for such exploitation subjects, in belief that in this atomic age such product will be well patronized. This belief appears well founded, judging by results of films already turned out and either already released or ready to go.

Reacting to their profitability, Pollexfen and Wisberg regularly interspersed sci-fi with their adventure titles:

Captive Women (1952), reteaming *Planet X*'s Clarke, Margaret Field and Schallert, took place in the New York City area, after The Bomb; *The Neanderthal Man* (1953) had the Jekyll and Hyde theme play out in California's High Sierras; *Port Sinister* (1953) was set on the Caribbean island of Port Royal that once sunk beneath the waves but occasionally comes up for air (now inhabited by giant crabs).

There was also a stretch when the names of Pollexfen and Wisberg turned up regularly in the Hollywood trades in regard to their lawsuit against Columbia and Sam Katzman: According to Jack and Aubrey, they submitted to "Jungle Sam" their original story *The Pirate and the Slave Girl* and he used it as the basis of his 1949 B-picture *Barbary Pirate*. The writers sailed to an easy victory in their (wait for it) *piracy* suit.

Pollexfen and Wisberg wrote, produced and also directed *Dragon's Gold* (1954), a Hong Kong-set adventure with small-scale, sometimes inept action scenes. After this, the two men unfriended each other and, especially with Wisberg, rancor ensued. "There was a lot of bitterness there," Pollexfen's longtime friend and associate Sue Bradford recalled for me. "Jack would express himself [complain] about Aubrey to me, or to Vy [Vy Russell, another close associate], and what have you, but I never heard Jack going around doing the sort of thing that apparently Aubrey *did* do, about Jack, with other people [badmouthing Pollexfen behind his back]."

Personal side note: In 1983 I wanted to separately interview both Pollexfen and Wisberg. Pollexfen agreed to be interviewed, even though he knew I was in touch with Wisberg. Wisberg agreed to be interviewed *until* he found out I was in touch with Pollexfen, at which point he abruptly gave me the brush-off.

Recalling the Pollexfen-Wisberg break-up, Vy told me, with a laugh, "Well, Aubrey had his problems!" She continued,

> Ilse Lahn, the charming, charming German lady who was with the Paul Kohner Agency, was the agent for both Jack and for Aubrey, and she thought highly of Aubrey and was quite a good friend of Aubrey's wife. She tried to smooth the troubled waters, but Aubrey had personality problems.

Burl Lampert, an employee and friend of Pollexfen's from 1996 'til 2002, adds, "Also, Jack hated Aubrey's wife with, to quote Stephanie Miller, 'the passion of a thousand white suns.'"

Pollexfen said that probably the main reason for the break-up was Wisberg's habit of getting into feuds

According to Robert Clarke, Pollexfen had a crush on actress Margaret Field and dropped about 30 pounds in hopes of making himself attractive to her. No dice. (Top photo: Field in *The Man from Planet X*; facing page photo, Clarke and Field in *Captive Women*.)

with people, including Ulmer[*] on *Planet X*; "He would be irritated if, say, a cameraman who'd worked for us once was not available on the next picture, and things of that nature. Very touchy." Perhaps joking, perhaps not, he added that another reason was the not-found-in-nature dialogue Wisberg tended to write for his script characters. And I know from a few phone conversations with Wisberg that he actually talked like his characters, and his brush-off letter to me sounded like it came from one of his characters. On pages 12 and 13 are a few examples of Wisberg at his windy worst:

---

[*] To be fair, it probably was easy to get into a scrap with Ulmer. Vy Russell thought he was charming, "but he could be difficult—at least, a lot of people seemed to think so. He was a little Hitler, you know [*laughs*]! You had to do it *his* way, which didn't always go down well with the actors. He never had trouble when he worked with my husband [d.p. John L. Russell]—Ulmer was always very flattering with anybody that he *respected*. But he also said his piece if he didn't think someone was quite up to snuff."

UNINTELLIGIBLE MAN: Aubrey Wisberg

By Tom Weaver

Picture a world in which Aubrey Wisberg never wrote dialogue. It's a world similar to our own, just a little better. Wisberg turned characters into walking thesauruses, speaking so ornately and unnaturally that Ed Wood's characters, by comparison, seem quite everyday in their speech. Ross Elliott co-starred as a teacher in a school for troubled girls in Wisberg-Pollexfen's *Problem Girls* (1953), shot at the Brunswig mansion on West Adams. Decades later when he talked to me, he still remembered one pearl of Wisberg dialogue word for word:

The way it read on the printed page, it wasn't even contracted: "I am—" not "I'm"…"I am anxious not to do anything that might interfere with my eventual certification by the State Board of Medicine." [*Laughs*] Okay?? It's a very awkward and stilted phraseology.

I said to [director E.A. DuPont], "Eddie, I can't say this!" He always had a cigarette drooping from his lower lip, and he looked at me through the smoke and with his eyes pointed over at Aubrey and said, "Tell *him*." So I went over to Aubrey and I said, "Aubrey, look, I can't *say* this, this is too stilted. Can't we loosen the line up?" He said, "You're playing a psychiatrist, you're playing a man who's been to college." I said, "Aubrey. I *graduated* from college. At the age of 19. I am *passing bright*, and I don't *talk* that way." There was a pause, and he said, "You *will* in *my* picture."

So I went back to Eddie and I told him, "I gotta do it, Eddie. You're a director, what do I *do* with it?" And he thought for a minute, and he had a slight German accent, and he said,

Aubrey Wisberg's reality chip was missing when it came to writing lifelike dialogue for the characters in his movies.

"I tell you vot…t'row it avay!" I said, "'T'row it avay'?! I can't *lift* it!"

You can find gems like that in many or maybe all of Aubrey's movies; for example, in *Dragon's Gold*, when one character talks about committing a killing, Chinese general Noel Cravat shrugs, "I refuse to be discommoded by your impulse." Margaret Field tells her father she saw the Man from Planet X and gets back, "Your statements have the tinge of fantasy!" Ad Aub-surdum.

The Neanderthal Man is a bottomless mine rich in nerdy nuggets. This Jekyll-and-Hyde-style monster movie is set in California's High Sierras, which stand "in brooding beauty, whose parallel one would have far to seek" (opening narration). Prof. Cliff Groves (Robert Shayne), a self-styled expert on the brain capacity of primitive man, is no Mensa in the People's Skills Dept.: At a meeting of the Naturalists Club, he mixes a presentation of his theories with insults directed at its members, prompting the head man to tell him,

> Prof. Groves, we must ask you not to invade these premises again, with theories which charity compels me to state have an aspect of lunacy.

In his home laboratory, Groves transforms a cat into a full-sized saber-tooth tiger which then escapes and causes some commotion. Zoologist Ross Harkness (Richard Crane) and a game warden (Robert Long) shoot and kill it, then announce this news to Groves, who feigns disbelief:

> Admit it was some practical joke which has misfired and I'll call upon my charity to overlook this dismal escapade.

Referring to the disappearance of the tiger carcass, Harkness spouts,

> There must be some logical cause and effect to this…this unholy adventure!

The best is yet to come: When Groves verbally spars with his fiancée Ruth, we get to hear lovers spatting the way they must do it on Planet Wisberg:

> **RUTH**: I want *you*. The man I once knew. The good companion, the cheerful friend. I want the happiness we once found in each other, I want… [*Pause*] What has come between us, Cliff? What is this unhappy work which absorbs you so much and is undermining your nervous system and making you such an intolerable sorehead?
>
> **GROVES** [*talking about the Naturalists Club members*]: A lot they know in their stupid obstinacy! In their peevishness of mind and soul! …You're no better than the rest of them. You're nothing but a vacuum of ego! Swelling! Ready to burst! Thinking your own empty desires to be all that there *is* in life! But there *are* more important things than your puny adoration of self!

"Aubrey was a very difficult man," said Vy Russell. "Talented in his own way…pompous…all of which is all right. But my *main* complaint was that his dialogue was *atrocious*. He over-wrote and over-wrote and over-wrote, and loved his own words. So there was always a little friction there, with whoever the other writers were, and with whoever the actors were that had to speak Aubrey's lines. They were precious in Aubrey's mind."

Wisberg, 78 years old and a resident of Manhattan, died of cancer at Lenox Hill Hospital on March 14, 1990.

The Making of
INDESTRUCTIBLE MAN

By Tom Weaver

Pollexfen's first movie after his break with Wisberg was *Indestructible Man*. Pollexfen told me that he wrote the first draft, with Vy and Sue helping on the second draft. But if you asked Sue, she'd say the movie was Pollexfen's idea and that she and Vy did the first draft. Ask Vy and you'd be told that the idea was Pollexfen's and the screenplay a joint effort. Pollexfen's name isn't in the on-screen writing credits because, as he said to me, he didn't want triple-capacity producer, director *and* writer credits on the movie; "I thought I would leave such credits to Chaplin and Welles."

Vy Russell and Sue Bradford were the wives of the cinematographers of some of the Wisberg-Pollexfen movies. In 1952, Sue (real name: Miriam Gretchen Sues), the daughter of cameraman Simmons Albert Sues, married d.p. William Bradford, whose list of credits stretched back into the 1930s. He'd done most of his work at Republic, including a dozen or more Roy Rogers Westerns, plus others with Don "Red" Barry, Bill Elliott, Allan Lane and Sunset Carson. Coincidentally, he'd also photographed Republic's *The Phantom Speaks* (1945), another tale of a mobster coming back to life for revenge—but supernaturally, not as a result of a scientific experiment as in *Indestructible Man*. Bradford's Republic stint was followed by a shorter one at Columbia, and then hundreds of TV episodes, mostly Western fare for Gene Autry's Flying A Pictures. Bradford shot Wisberg-Pollexfen's *Port Sinister* and *Return to Treasure Island*.

A native of Galveston, Texas, Vy married John L. Russell in 1933, when he was an assistant cameraman at Columbia. "Jack" Russell was born into the movie business with *both* his parents involved in making pictures; his mom L. Case Russell was one of the early screenwriters. For Wisberg-Pollexfen, Russell was behind the camera on *The Man from Planet X*,

According to *Video Watchdog* magazine's Tim Lucas, "With bottles of hooch in nearly every shot, *Indestructible Man* looks like a dive bar smells." Lon Chaney says he'll drink to *that*.

Sword of Venus (1953) and *Problem Girls*—and now, on loanout from Republic, Pollexfen's *Indestructible Man*. Like William Bradford, Russell had a résumé heavy on B-pictures and TV Western fare, but his list of credits was also dotted with better titles: Orson Welles' *Macbeth* (1948), Frank Borzage's *Moonrise* (1948) and Alfred Hitchcock's *Psycho* (1960), receiving an Academy Award nomination for the latter. For Hitch he also photographed scores of *Alfred Hitchcock Presents* and *Alfred Hitchcock Hour* episodes.

Sue and Vy first worked for Pollexfen on a volunteer basis, during the making of *Man from Planet X*. (Sue hadn't yet married Bradford but they were already seeing each other.) The women knew that the phones would probably go unanswered in the Wisberg-Pollexfen office during *Planet X* production, so they offered to pitch in. Sue recalled, "Jack being Jack, of course, he said, 'Well, I don't know about that. Aubrey and I would rather have blondes.' So…Vy and I spent one whole day trying to become blonde." Despite their best efforts, both came out with hair that was different shades of blonde-*red*. Sue laughingly recalled Pollexfen's reaction when they arrived for Day 1 of office work and he saw them for the first time as "blondes": "Jack didn't let on then, but he told me afterwards that it really scared him because when he saw what we'd done, he figured that *both* Bill and Jack were going to be absolutely furious [*laughs*]! He thought to himself, 'Oh my God, Jack and Bill are gonna *kill* me!'"

For *Indestructible Man*, no director that Pollexfen wanted was available, so since he had his own Directors Guild card, he decided to take the helm. For the title role he selected Lon Chaney, the top dog horror star at Universal in the 1940s. By the 1950s, the actor had slipped from stardom to the ranks to supporting player, even in the horror movie genre he used to rule. Despite being a take-off on Chaney's own *The Wolf Man* (1941), *Bride of the Gorilla* (1951) relegated Chaney to the thankless role of a jungle police commissioner. Even at Universal where he had once ruled the monster roost, he got fifth billing and a mute henchman character to play in *The Black Castle* (1952). He did however head the castlist of *Indestructible Man*, the *only* 1950s movie in which he gets top billing. He hadn't been star-billed in a Hollywood movie since 1948, when his name topped the on-screen castlist of Monogram's *16 Fathoms Deep* (and undeservedly so; Lon had a smallish role as that movie's villain). Chaney wouldn't be top-billed again until the mid-1960s' *Spider Baby, House of the Black Death* and *Dr. Terror's Gallery of Horrors*. Chaney is 48

In 1952, Chaney clowned with co-star Paula Corday in publicity photos for *The Black Castle*, a Universal horror flick partly shot on the Phantom Stage built for Lon's dad's *The Phantom of the Opera*.

in *Indestructible Man*, one year older than his dear old Dad ever got.

"Select Casey Adams as *Indestructible Man*" was the title of a November 12, 1954, *Variety* blurb that gives the wrong (but funny!) impression that Adams would be playing the monstrous title role. The actor had spent most of his movie career to date at 20th Century-Fox where he'd signed a seven-way contract as test director, dialogue director, director, scenarist, lyricist, composer and actor. I don't know what he did there other than "actor," but he did it in some major movies—to name just three, *What Price Glory?* (1952) with James Cagney, *Destination Gobi* (1953) with Richard Widmark and *Niagara* (1953) with Marilyn Monroe. For *Niagara*, cast and crew traveled to Niagara Falls, where a stark naked Monroe came uninvited from her hotel room to Adams', jumped on his bed and asked him to help her learn her lines.

For Adams it was quite a step down from these Fox movies to freelance roles in *The Monster That Challenged the World* (1957) and *Indestructible Man*, but he told me

Angels Flight has been seen in dozens of movies and TV episodes dating back to the silent era. Pollexfen once claimed that he filmed in this section of L.A. because he knew the neighborhood would eventually be destroyed in the name of urban development: "Very prescient of me, wouldn't you say?"

he enjoyed the latter because he "*loved* working with Lon Chaney!"

Signed the same day (November 11) as Adams, Marian Carr had recently been called the Marilyn Monroe of television by columnist Erskine Johnson, who reported that she'd been "overheating the tubes" on series like *Four Star Playhouse*. He quoted Carr as saying that she'd missed out on many TV roles because casting directors "seem to think I'm too sexy for living rooms." Carr began her movie career by signing with RKO in late 1945; they put her to work in Leon Errol comedy shorts, in *It's a Wonderful Life* (as the bride of newly wealthy plastic manufacturer Frank "Heehaw!!" Albertson) and in a couple of Lawrence Tierney crime dramas, *San Quentin* and *The Devil Thumbs a Ride*. After a career gap of several years (marriage and motherhood), Carr's first movie was the low-budget Mounties adventure *Northern Patrol* (1953) with Marian as a gunfighter(!). She also did crime flicks immediately before and after *Indestructible Man*: Shot in September-October 1954, *Cell 2455, Death Row*, based on the criminal career of Caryl Chessman, featured Carr as William Campbell's girlfriend who wants him to go straight. Then right after *Indestructible* she appeared in *Kiss Me Deadly* with Ralph Meeker as Mike Hammer.

Vy said that Pollexfen was loyal to actors and, following Chaney, Adams and Carr, the rest of the *Indestructible Man* castlist bears this out, with supporting roles played by Ross Elliott (*Problem Girls*), Ken Terrell (*Sword of Venus, Port Sinister, Captain Kidd and the Slave Girl, Return to Treasure Island, Daughter of Dr. Jekyll*), Robert Shayne (*The Neanderthal Man*), Marjorie Stapp (*Problem Girls, Port Sinister, Sword of Venus, Daughter of Dr. Jekyll*) and Roy Engel (*The Man from Planet X, Dragon's Gold*). Stuart Randall, who plays Capt. Lauder, was another Pollexfen regular; he may have played his best role in Wisberg-Pollexfen's post-apocalyptic sci-fi *Captive Women*, as the ruthless head of the Upriver tribe. In 1951's *The Hoodlum* Randall played the "pinch-crazy" cop who, prior to the start of the movie, put Lawrence Tierney away for five years; Randall, who leads the sewer manhunt in *Indestructible Man*, leads an almost-as-nasty city dump manhunt for

Tierney at *The Hoodlum*'s end.

Pollexfen arranged to shoot interiors at Jerry Fairbanks Studios, and picked exterior locations alongside Vy Russell, who told me:

> We had a lot of location work on *Indestructible Man*, including the wonderful Angels Flight, which I think shows up well in the film. Also the Bradbury Building, which is lovely, a *beautiful* building. I think Jack Pollexfen was one of the first to use that as a picture set. He *loves* Los Angeles, and the man is loaded with the history of it. Well, he's an expert on anything—name it and Pollexfen is an authority on it. But particularly Los Angeles. I tramped the streets of Los Angeles with Pollexfen looking for locations and doing this, that and the other thing, and his knowledge of its background is remarkable.

"I always liked working on location," Pollexfen told me. "Certainly, on a tight budget, you can get production values you can't afford on a studio set."

On November 12, Geoffrey M. Shurlock of the Production Code Administration advised Pollexfen in a letter that he (Shurlock) had read the draft script for his proposed production *Indestructible Man* and was "pleased to report that it is basically acceptable under the provisions of the Production Code." One wonders how pleased Shurlock would be had he known that Pollexfen hadn't waited for his seal of approval: *Indestructible Man* began production on November 11, the day before Shurlock wrote it! Jerry Fairbanks Studios at 6052 Sunset, where the interior scenes were done, had been used for the shooting of industrial films in the 1940s; several Paramount shorts series (Popular Science, Unusual Occupations, Speaking of Animals) were also made there in that era. In the 1950s, it was home to the producers of TV series, *Cowboy G-Men* for one. If there were records documenting *Indestructible Man*'s day-to-day production, I don't know where to begin to look for them. Casey Adams had a memory of most of the movie being made in sequence. He was there and I wasn't but to me this doesn't seem at all likely.

Part of the joy of *Indestructible Man* is seeing Los Angeles back in the day, grime, sleaze, warts and all; John Russell's camera works like a magnet, picking up plenty of squalid details. (The *Indestructible Man* pressbook calls the once-fashionable downtown Bunker Hill section of L.A., where parts of it were made, "now a blighted area.") The burlesque house where Eva (Carr) bumps and grinds—always off-camera—is established via exterior shots of a 6th and Main theater built before the turn of the 20th century. Early in its history, it had a series of names (the Burbank Theater, Morosco's Burbank Theater, etc.) and for a stretch it hosted legit plays with some distinguished players, including Richard Bennett and Julia Dean. (Dean, many years and many wrinkles later, played the spooky recluse Mrs. Farren in 1944's *The Curse of the Cat People*.) By the 1930s it was a newsreel theater and by the 1950s it had yet more handles, including the Burbank Burlesque Theatre and the New Follies Theatre.*

Especially fun to watch is the high-angle footage (undoubtedly shot via hidden camera) of Chaney's "Butcher" Benton walking amidst dozens of other pedestrians on crowded Hill Street. Hands in his pockets, he looks "like any normal person—on his way to work, or on his way home," as narrator Chasen says of Benton as this footage plays. One or two drugstore cowboys, leaning on the wall of a store, catch sight of the actor and bird-dog him as he passes; when Chaney crosses the street, a guy crossing the other way appears to turn and gesture toward him. If you're enough of a Monster Kid Nerd, it's fun to see Angelenos' genuine reaction to having the creature (from so many monster movies) walk among them.

(A tip for fans: In order to stay absorbed and immersed in the universe of this movie, tell yourself that everyone who gapes is not recognizing Chaney, they're reacting with surprise to the sight of a guy who looks exactly like the just-executed "Butcher" Benton!)

Benton boards one of the Angels Flight railway cars, which (one dissolve later) is rolling the two steep uphill blocks toward Olive Street and the Hillcrest Hotel. Sue recalled that the day's work at Angels Flight "was somewhat difficult because of onlookers."

Underworld lawyer Paul Lowe hangs his shady shingle in L.A.'s splendid Bradbury Building, just a block from Angels Flight.† Today (2014) it's "the oldest commercial building remaining in the central city and one of Los Angeles' unique treasures" (the Los Angeles Conservancy website). Benton drops Squeamy from the top floor into the court and still manages to get away scot-free, quite a feat considering the number of witnesses there'd be in such a busy building. But this is nitpicking: The murders in other movies of this type

---

* When we see a long shot of the burlesque house at night, the name Betty Rowland—Ball of Fire is on the lit-up marquee. One of the original Minsky's girls, Rowland—nicknamed "Ball of Fire" because of her long, flaming red hair—is still with us at nearly 100. Watch her strut her stuff on YouTube.

† Actually, all three of these locations—the burlesque theater, Angels Flight and the Bradbury Building—were in the same general area, not far from the city's Skid Row.

The Bradbury Building, 304 South Broadway. Squeamy Ellis gets what's coming to him in its skylighted court.

almost invariably take place in remote and eerie spots in the dead of night, but "Butcher" Benton operates out in the open and *then* some, audaciously striking in bustling parts of L.A. in broad daylight, and with blaring Albert Glasser music seeming to call *additional* attention to his mayhem. The "in your face" ferocity of his rampages is refreshing.

The script calls for a small crowd to gather in the lobby around Squeamy's body; in the movie, comically, the actors and extras involved are looking almost *straight* down, which gives the impression that their feet must be in the blood of the splattered Squeamy! After a dissolve or two to convey the passage of time, Chasen and Lauder arrive on the scene and some of those extras *are still there*, still giving the impression they're practically on top of the corpse, still with placid, pleasant expressions on their faces, rocking their heads back and forth like Louvre visitors spending a lazy afternoon contemplating the Mona Lisa's smile.

Indestructible Man was apparently shot in a mad rush—Vy Russell called it "an 18-out-of-24-hours deal"—and perhaps Pollexfen wasn't the ideal director for such a whirlwind schedule. "Jack was a better producer than he was a director," Sue told me with a laugh. "I've said this to him too! Lon was very strong and Lon kinda wanted to 'take over.' He wanted to make suggestions and so forth, which he *did*." She continued,

> Lon was very friendly. I remember sitting and talking with him. He grew up in the business, so as kids we knew a lot of the same people, being kids of motion picture people. And he was fine. The only thing is, he was *so* strong that… [*Pause*] My feeling is that, lots of times, Jack wouldn't know quite how to control him, or get him to do what way *he* thought [Pollexfen didn't know how to get Chaney to do things the way Pollexfen thought they should be done]. That's kind of vague in my mind, why I have that overall impression. I know Lon wasn't being difficult from the standpoint of trying to be unpleasant about it.

Vy's memory of Chaney was that he was "very professional. Very nice man. Kept to himself, but always on deck. No problems. He was always a professional." Casey Adams told me Chaney was "a pussycat" (see Adams interview starting on page 157) and Ross Elliott called him "really a fascinating guy. Nice guy, just as nice as could be. Worked *very* hard— he *didn't* play. *He* worked, he did it. And when he was in character and doing it, he was *scary*!"

In 1988, when Mike Brunas and I interviewed Robert Shayne at his home, we asked about Chaney and the heretofore affable actor became guarded in his tone, tersely noting his disapproval of actors who imbibe while working. "Chaney could handle dialogue reasonably well," Pollexfen told me. "Of course, a talkative monster would tend to be ridiculous. I found him intelligent, probably more so than most actors. He warned me before we started shooting, 'Don't make any changes in dialogue, or add new dialogue, after lunch!'—which he drank down rather liberally."

Pollexfen and Burl Lampert watched *Indestructible Man* several times together, and in that very informal atmosphere, Pollexfen sang a more lurid tune: "According to Jack, after 'lunch' Mr. Chaney could barely speak or stand up, he was so loaded," Lampert told me.

Did Sue and Vy fib to me about Chaney always being professional, or did Pollexfen fib to Lampert about Chaney being hammered? Your guess is as good as mine.

Chaney's bottle-nipping rep have probably made more than a few fans wonder if the actor was a handful on *Indestructible Man*. But according to Sue and Vy, the trouble came instead from an unexpected source.

"Lon just wanted to be helpful. And, after all, he was a pro," said Sue. "Which is more than I can say for the young lady [Marian Carr]!" She elaborated,

> I don't know what her problem was. In later years, we talked about it, guessed about it. Maybe she was "on" something. She wasn't temperamental in a way like she thought she was the queen bee or something, but she'd get upset. And you can't really afford a lot of that when

Benton (Chaney) with the girl he mistakenly thinks is *his* girl: Eva (Marian Carr), a sweet-faced goody-two-shoes who happens to work as a stripper.

you're shootin' on a shoestring.

She got mad one day when we were shooting on the stage, and I don't remember what she got mad about. But she got mad about something, and all of a sudden they were all set up to shoot and she wasn't there. "Where's Marian?", and she's not there. So somebody went to knock on the little dressing room door, and she was upset about something, and she wouldn't come out. And she wouldn't talk to anybody, "Go away!" and so forth. Everybody was ready and waiting to do the scene. Finally she said she would let *me* in to talk to her. God knows why [*laughs*], but she said she would! Whatever it was, I don't even remember, she was all upset about something that didn't amount to a *damn*. So she cost us time.

"I didn't think she was that good, really," Casey Adams told *VideoScope* magazine's Ronald L. Smith. "She was very difficult to work with; she didn't quite give as much as I like to get from fellow performers. …I think they were hoping she was going to be another Marilyn Monroe, but that never happened."

"Marian Carr was a very attractive and talented lady," said Vy, "but insecure in this potboiler of a movie that she wasn't sure about. So she had some problems."

At some point during production, *some*thing went amiss—but try as I have, I've never been able to nail down the story. If I'd asked Jack Pollexfen in 1983 when I did my first interview with him, he would have remembered; he was then "only" 75 and his memory was good. But in those Dark Ages of Monster Kid Scholarship, there was no way for me to know that there *had* been problems. By the time I figured out that things had gone haywire production-wise, he was much older and his memory wasn't 100 percent any more.

Still photographs like this one attest to the fact that the moviemakers did shoot the scene of Benton storming police HQ and adding Paul Lowe's name to his death ledger. "*Indestructible Man* rises above its no-budget roots," wrote *VideoScope* magazine's David Alexander Nahmod. "This is one of the rare times when Lon is actually scary."

Vy and Sue were both very sharp when I interviewed them in 1996, and both remembered that the picture ran into trouble, but neither could remember what the trouble *was*.* Sue recalled that the financing collapsed partway through; "I remember the day, on the stage, when Pollexfen told Vy, Jack Russell and me what had happened."

Many movies run into money troubles or other difficulties in midstream and suspend production; to name one oldie as an example, Bela Lugosi's *Bride of the Monster*. Like *Indestructible Man*, that Ed Wood production began shooting in the fall of 1954 but then the Hollywood trades reported that it had shut down; they also ran items in March of 1955 when production resumed; and so the story is well-documented. But the news of *Indestructible Man*'s travails seems not to have made the trades. What makes things even more baffling is the fact that the movie apparently *was* completed (or close) during that first round of shooting—and that the first-time-around version had an entirely different ending than the film as released.

The *Indestructible Man* we know, and the 91-page script in this book, are fairly identical right up to page 70. At that point in the script, Benton takes a nighttime drive to a sump pit where he's stashed the armored car and the $600,000. He recovers the loot, secretes it in a cave, and then goes hunting for Paul Lowe.

Next in the script comes the description of the

---

* Probably part of Vy and Sue's confusion was the fact that *Indestructible Man* wasn't the only Pollexfen picture to hit a snag. Ross Elliott, co-star of the Wisberg-Pollexfen *Problem Girls*, recalled for me that they were right in the middle of working on a scene when suddenly somebody said "*Cut!*" and, according to Elliott, "*bingo*, that was it [the movie shut down even though the movie wasn't finished]. That's how tight that budget was." The producers were out of money and production needed to end that very second. Unfortunately for *Problem Girls*, the never-finished scene was the capper for the picture, which now ends abruptly and with some plot points unexplained!

The Butcher just wants revenge. Is that so wrong?

scene that every Indestructible Fan knows was filmed and wants to see, if it still exists anywhere, which it surely doesn't. For fans of Chaney's father, *London After Midnight* (1927) is the Holy Grail; for fans of Lon Jr., it might be the "Butcher Opens a Can of Whoop-Ass" police station scene from *Indestructible Man*. It begins with Benton arriving at the police station's parking garage and approaching the mayor's elevator. The police elevator operator frowns and begins questioning him—and then realizes who he's talking to. A "wipe" abruptly ends this scene and begins the next, with Benton exiting the elevator on the building's "jail floor"; inside the elevator we can see the operator's crumpled body.

The next shot is of the cellblock with Lowe in a cell, Chasen and Eva talking to him through the bars. Three other policemen are in the room. Suddenly there's the sound of gunshots, and the Butcher bursts through the door. One cop opens fire and gets knocked to the floor.

The second cop (with a tear gas gun) is also clobbered, and then the third. Chasen, gun in hand, is holding his ground when Eva unexpectedly gets between him and the Indestructible Man. Chasen pushes her aside and then gets pushed aside himself by the Butcher.

Lowe knows the jig is up: Pressing himself against the back wall of the cell, he babbles, "Benton—I'm your friend—I didn't double-cross you…" From the script: "Butcher shoves outstretched hands against bars—they give way—Butcher's huge frame—his hands still outstretched—blots out view of Paul as he continues toward him." As we watch Eva trying to revive Chasen, we hear the off-screen Lowe wailing, his voice rising to a shriek and then breaking off.

Okay, do you want to see that, or *London After Midnight*?

The cellblock action continues with the Butcher carrying away a struggling, screaming Eva. The cops later trace them to the cave and converge on the area armed with flame throwers, tear gas guns and bazookas. Inside the cave, Benton and Eva talk, and the Lennie-like Benton is shaken up to find that, for Eva, the romantic embers have gone cold now that he's a monster. In hopes of rescuing Eva, Chasen slips into the cave and shoots Benton in the face with tear gas. With Benton reeling, Chasen grabs Eva and half-drags her out a different cave entrance.

Now the cops are free to go to town on the Butcher with the flame throwers and bazookas. He rolls around on the cave floor to extinguish the flames, then flees out that other cave entrance. Roaring with rage, he starts chasin' Chasen and Eva. Chasen *wants* Benton to pursue him, pushing Eva into a patrol car and driving away; obligingly, Benton gets into his pick-up truck and follows. The procession (Chasen and Eva followed by Benton, who is followed by all the patrol cars) winds up at a nearby electrical station. Chasen and Eva get out of the car and run in the gate. Benton climbs out of his truck but seems reluctant to enter. "You'll never get her, Butcher!" Chasen yells, taunting the Indestructible Man, who comes charging after them.

Chasen and Eva get up onto a catwalk, and as Eva runs to safety, Chasen goes into a control house and activates a gantry crane. With Benton approaching, Chasen jumps for a grappling hook and swings to safety as the fast-moving gantry crane slams into the catwalk and there is a tremendous flash that spells the end for the Butcher.

In the final scene of the script, Chasen is at the burlesque house, studying a cardboard cutout of Eva, buying a ticket at the box office and, with "a slight smile" starting to appear on his face, heading inside. **THE END**.

Many or perhaps *all* of these scenes were put on film and then scrapped, which is mystifying. Usually when producers run out of money, they end up with "half" a movie; how could the *Indestructible* crew run out of money and then end up with *more* than a full movie (the first version plus then a second version with many new scenes)? Proving that Benton's assault on the police station was shot, there are at least two stills of Chaney on that set, and Pollexfen, Vy, Sue and Ross Elliott all had fragmentary memories of the scene where Benton kills Lowe. Pollexfen recalled the cell bars being rubber. Elliott amusingly reminisced:

> We did that scene on a little sound stage made up like a prison. That was at the time when I first started to wear a hairpiece, a small "front piece" that would go in the center in the front. It was rather hot, and I will never forget, as he

came at me, the damn hairpiece came off right in the middle of a shot! The sweat was pouring down, and Chaney was so convincing, and the hairpiece slipped off!

Also shot, according to Vy, Sue and Casey Adams, were scenes in the cave. Sue recalled that they were done in the famous "cave" in Griffith Park's Bronson Canyon (naturally) and that they were working at night, she and Vy consulting their script by flashlight. A bit of this cave footage *is* in the finished film: In the sewer, when Benton is being roasted by the flame thrower, notice that the background is no longer the smooth man-made walls of the sewer, but *cave* walls.

Presumably every scene that's **in** the movie but *not* **in the script in this book** was shot when production again got underway: Lowe visiting Benton on Death Row, the first scene of Chasen and Capt. Lauder, Chasen and Eva's hamburger drive-in dates, Lowe's confession to the police. The sewer scenes were definitely filmed during the second go-round; Casey Adams recalls that they had to be shot *twice*. To make room for all this new material, some footage had to go; this includes the cave scene and all shots of Eva at the power station.

In the finished film, partly as a result of all the re-shooting, the narration features bits of misinformation, characters say and do inexplicable things, the murders of Joe and Squeamy are out of order…in other words, the simple-enough-for-a-child storyline of *Indestructible Man* had morphed into one of the milestones in the history of Head-Scratching Schlock Cinema. Some of the goofs that viewers will notice:

🪦 At the end of the Death Row scene between Benton and Lowe, narrator Chasen calls this final meeting of longtime associates Benton and Lowe the *first* meeting of Benton and Lowe.

🪦 Benton visits Eva in her dressing room, says nothing (obviously), and leaves. Why, then, does Eva rush to a pay phone to call Squeamy Ellis to warn him that Benton is on his way over to kill him? And then run out to the Hillcrest Hotel, where Squeamy lives, to try and save him?

⚔ According to narrator Chasen, the revenge-minded Benton "thought of Squeamy and Joe first. He was saving Paul Lowe for last." But after Benton kills Joe, narrator Chasen returns with, "[Benton] thought about Paul Lowe, the next man on his list." What happened to "saving Paul Lowe for last"?

⚔ Benton kills Joe, then catches up with Squeamy in the Bradbury Building and drops him to his death. Summoned to the scene, Police Capt. Lauder orders a stakeout on Joe, and Chasen pipes up, "I'd like to talk to Joe." Haven't you forgotten something, guys? That...ummmm...Joe is already *dead*?!

⚔ Investigating the killing of Squeamy, Dick charges into Capt. Lauder's office holding a "report on Dr. Bradshaw, owner of the station wagon." Ummmm… yes, Dr. Bradshaw owned a station wagon…but Benton didn't take it. He left Dr. Bradshaw's place on foot and *kept* traveling on foot until he stole Carney's car. How did Dr. Bradshaw and his station wagon get on Chasen's radar?

⚔ Behind the wheel of his car, Lowe hears a radio broadcaster talk about the murder of Joe…repeat, *the murder of Joe*…and drives to the Hall of Justice. There, Eva tells him that Benton killed Squeamy and Joe. Lowe responds with shock, "Joe *too*?" Joe was the one you *knew* about, idiot!

⚔ After Benton meets his electrical end, Chasen talks to Capt. Lauder at headquarters and says of Eva, "I called the hospital an hour ago. She'd gone." Hospital? What was she doing in the hospital?

Reading the script helps you understand how some (*some*!) of these blunders happened. In the script, Benton *does* take Bradshaw's station wagon. He *does* tell Eva he intends to kill Squeamy, Joe and Lowe. Joe and Squeamy *are* killed in that order. In the movie, we see Lowe at the wheel of his car as narrator Chasen tells us that Lowe is hearing a news report about the death of Joe. But in the script (page 65), there's no narration and we, along with Lowe, hear the news report:

> [A] reliable source informs me that one man— a superhuman fiend—is believed responsible for this trail of destruction from San Francisco to Los Angeles. A blood-chilling sequel to this afternoon's murder of Squeamy Ellis is the statement of a witness that the killer… Get this—the witness claims the killer is Charles— the Butcher—Benton—a man who was legally executed in San Quentin yesterday afternoon!

So in the script, when Lowe gets to the police station, his line "Joe *too*?" is the natural response. The talk of Eva's hospitalization makes sense in the script, because throughout several preceding pages she was roughly manhandled, both at the police station and in the cave, by Benton.

Considering all that's wrong with the movie storyline-wise, it's funny to learn that at the time of production, the glitch most upsetting to Vy and Sue was—Marian Carr's shoes! While shooting the power station scene, the two ladies watched Carr and Casey Adams climbing the ladder to the gantry crane when, Sue told me,

> we were horrified to note that Marian had on flat-heeled shoes instead of the high-heeled black shoes that she had been wearing in previous scenes. We hurriedly conferred with [d.p.] Jack Russell to find out if the shoes showed prominently. They did. It was good action, we couldn't re-shoot, we were racing against losing the light. So Vy and I sat on the curb and scanned the script for the first chance for the heroine to change shoes. It turned out to be the first scene to be shot the next morning [on the police station set]. We added some dialogue about her having broken her heel. The next morning while they were setting up on stage, I went down Hollywood Blvd. to the nearest shoe store, waited for it to open and bought the flat-heeled shoes which you see her accept in the police station.

Once the production chaos had come to an end and the movie as we know it was put together, "I was reasonably satisfied with it," Pollexfen told me. "I thought I did about as good as job of directing as a number of directors we'd used—but I was *not* as good as an Ulmer or a DuPont!" He later wrote me (in a letter dated October 31—Halloween!—but no year) that the *Indestructible Man* budget was about $40,000. "Studio bookkeeping is a disaster," he continued. "I found that I did much better on cash deals. The budgets of [*The Neanderthal Man, Indestructible Man, Daughter of Dr. Jekyll* and *Monstrosity*], below the line, generally ran between $40,000 and $65,000."

Arthur Shields is about to begin his "werewolf" transformation in Pollexfen's *Daughter of Dr. Jekyll* (1957).

Allied Artists began distributing *Indestructible Man* in March 1956 (see Dr. Robert J. Kiss's "*Indestructible Man*—The Release" on pages 159-160 for details). Apparently Allied was happy with the picture and with Pollexfen, and Pollexfen was happy with Allied, because on October 15, 1956, Pollexfen announced the formation of Film Venturers, Inc., a new indie unit whose first production *Daughter of Dr. Jekyll* would be made for Allied release. (Several years earlier, Pollexfen was a writer on Columbia's *The Son of Dr. Jekyll*.) On *Daughter* he again surrounded himself with people he knew: his agent Ilse Lahn as associate producer,* Edgar G. Ulmer as director, Vy and Sue as uncredited production assistants, Marjorie Stapp and Rita Greene (or is it Green?) in the cast and Ken Terrell stunt-doubling Mr. Hyde. Was 11 Pollexfen's lucky number?: *Daughter* began shooting on 11/11/56, two years to the day after *Indestructible Man*'s 11/11/54 start date. According to a January 25, 1957, *Variety* news blurb, Pollexfen had scheduled *Vampire Planet* as the second film on his Film Venturers slate, with production to start early in March. *That* movie never got off the launch pad.†

In May 1958 *Variety* announced that Pollexfen had obtained exclusive western hemisphere rights to Dyadicscope, "film process developed in Holland by which outsize figures, people or animals, can be blown up to giant proportions or shrunk to a few inches in height. …Process uses two camera lenses to produce, through a system of mirrors and prisms, two separate images on a single frame of film." The process was going to make its bow in Pollexfen's *The Astonishing 12-Inch People* and *The Brain Snatchers*, both planned for

---

* According to Lahn's 1992 *Variety* obit, one of the movies she, Pollexfen and Wisberg produced was (wait for it)…*Bride of Frankenstein*!

† Around this same time, Aubrey Wisberg was also promising future sci-fi flicks that never eventuated: In August 1956, he and director Jean Yarbrough were in the midst of making *The Women of Pitcairn Island*—yet another "descendants of literary characters" movie—and they announced that scripts had finished for Wisberg-Yarbrough Productions' *Panic in Outer Space* and *The Invisible Monster*.

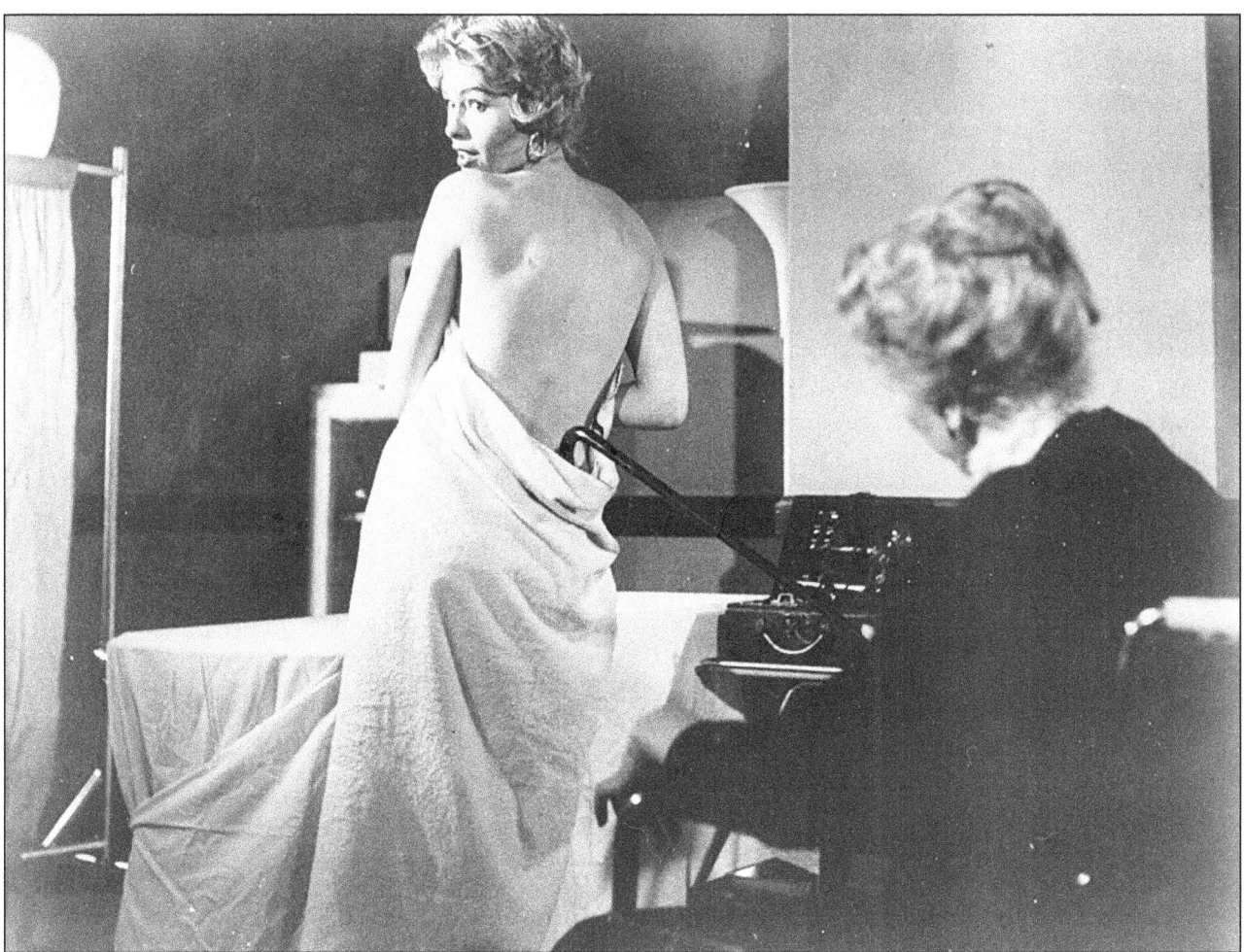

In *Monstrosity*, housekeeper Judy Bamber giggles, "I've got the same measurements as Marilyn Monroe"—unaware that her 80-year-old employer Marjorie Eaton is shopping for a hot body into which her brain can be transplanted! Pollexfen says it was the worst picture he was ever involved with, and the only one that never climbed into the profit column.

summer starts. I have no idea if there was ever any such process and I have even less of an idea what the word *dyadic* means even after reading the definition in the dictionary. In fact, *especially* after reading the definition in the dictionary. *The Brain Snatchers* eventually came to the screen as *Monstrosity*, made circa 1960 by Pollexfen and a crew largely made up of amateurs, and unleashed in 1963. "The name describes it," said Pollexfen.

After *Monstrosity*, Pollexfen went into semi-retirement and, on March 23, 1964, married for the first time: In Ukiah, California, Pollexfen, 55, and Lee Hecker, 49-year-old creative director of the California Wine Advisory Board, were spliced in a double-ring ceremony in the chambers of a Superior Court judge. They would make their home in the Mill Valley area where Pollexfen had grown up. According to Burl Lampert,

At first, they rented several wonderful homes; Lee once showed me a few. "We knew we'd find the right place," Lee told me. Then they found a house on Bulkley Avenue in Sausalito, on the cliff that overlooks the old Trident Restaurant where Janis Joplin held court. It was over 100 years old, with a view east past Oakland to the furthest mountains, and a fantastic view across the Bay, with Angel Island in the foreground. They gutted the place but retained many parts, such as the 12-foot-plus doors, and also recycled wood that was removed. They created a very humble but beautiful home, full of light—which Jack, the world's most avid reader, appreciated in particular. By all accounts it was a terrific retirement.

Early on, they provided room and board for the young sculptress Jenny Read while she studied, her parents being friends of Jack and Lee. She wrote of Jack and Lee in her journal—much about the gourmet cooking that Jack did. "How we dine!" she wrote her parents. (In 1976, after Jenny moved out and into her own place in San Francisco, she was murdered. The crime was solved only recently, and the murderer is now in prison forever.)

When Jack started having serious trouble walking, a result of diabetes, he decided he wanted to sell one more script, so he set up a tape recorder and dictated. The tapes were then transcribed by a young man that Jack referred to as "Newport News" because he came from East Coast money. This was in the early '90s. As Jack's eyesight dwindled, they hired a series of "readers" who would read back the dictation.

(Lampert met Pollexfen by becoming his reader. He shares more memories of Pollexfen beginning on page 29.)

Pollexfen's diabetes cost him a leg; toward the end, he was blind or nearly blind. ("It was the loss of his reading ability that really broke Jack," says Lampert.) Despite these challenges, it looked for a while as though *he* was going to be the indestructible man and outlive every member of that movie's cast and crew, not to mention the casts and crews of most of his *other* movies.

For Monster Kids, the highlight of director Joe Dante's *Looney Tunes: Back in Action* (2003) was the Area 52 scene featuring, among other icons, the Fabulous Fifties' Robby the Robot, Robot Monster, a Metaluna Mutant, a Fiend Without a Face—and the Man from Planet X, Pollexfen's first sci-fi creation. *Looney Tunes* premiered on November 14, 2003; about a week later, 95-year-old Pollexfen began a bout with pneumonia. It soon ended with his death at Kaiser Permanente Hospital in San Rafael.

"Jack's pneumonia came on quickly but he never complained," the Pollexfens' acquaintance Steve (I've forgotten his last name) emailed me at the time. "It was peaceful for him and he did not suffer. His wonderful wife Lee always gave him the best of care in every way and their love really stood the test of time."

"He was the sweetest man in the world," Lee told obit writer Mika Edwards of the *Marin Independent Journal*. "He was such a joy to live with."

And Pollexfen's sci-fi films continue to live on, especially *The Man from Planet X* and *Indestructible Man*. In a Turner Classic Movies website essay on the latter, Nathaniel Thompson wrote, "[G]iven its resilience today and fond status among Chaney fans, it's fair to say that this film has actually proven far more indestructible than its resuscitated title character."

"Jack certainly never got the recognition he deserved in life—he did not have the ego required," said Burl Lampert. "But he really delighted in knowing that his work survives."

Many decades in the past, Jack and Lee dated but he was then too old for her. She married a jazz musician but Jack still carried a torch. After the musician's death in a boating accident and a reasonable mourning period, they had a wonderful romance that quickly culminated in marriage.

INDISPENSABLE MAN

By Burl Lampert

In 1996, Burl Lampert took a job as a "reader" for the now vision-impaired Jack Pollexfen and they hit it off immediately, with Lampert becoming one of the bright spots in the latter years of Pollexfen's life. Lampert here shares a few memories:

I came to Jack from an ad for a reader, which turned out to be reading Jack's transcripts of his scripts-in-progress back to him. Almost immediately, I found pages and sections of script stashed everywhere—under beds, in drawers, behind books. It took two years, but I collated them down to about 30 finished scripts and parts of about 40 others. Several of the older ones were hilarious: more literature than filmable script, but very much of Jack's unique sense of humor.

It was in reading all these scripts to him that I developed a "stock company" of voices, and a few sound effects, that Jack so enjoyed. We would develop voices to fit characters. It was a totally new creative experience for him, and he got such a kick out of it. I performed all these scripts over and over. And over. And over...but rehearsal pays off, and when I finally recorded several of them, they were, if I may toot my proverbial horn, hilarious. It was as if he had actually filmed them: When I was not there, he'd lie in bed listening to them endlessly, and seeing the action in his head. It must have been so fulfilling for him then, to be able to experience his tales exactly as he'd wished.

Jack was trying to write a sexy screwball comedy. He had such titles as *The Girl Who Dipped Her Toe in Champagne* and *The Girl Who Lost Her Nightie in Paris*. He also continued tightening earlier scripts, many of which were quite good. He did a series of comedies with Dr. Frankenstein at the center...*Frankenstein's Mother-in-Law*, *Frankenstein's Girls*, etc. He rethought Baron von Frankenstein as a sort of white-bread nebbish, and sent him on some very funny adventures. For *Frankenstein's Girls*, the best in the series, I brought in a bunch of actors and we made a recording of it, in character.

Jack and I also watched movies together, most often Billy Wilder films—Jack worshipped Billy Wilder. We also watched Jack's films. He had only two when I started with him, but I found 25 or so others over the years. He'd give the most delicious commentary... such as, in *Indestructible Man*, the actress playing the barfly was constantly smoking pot! Jack didn't mind her reeking of weed, because she performed perfectly

Lee and Jack Pollexfen and Jack's caregiver.

Pollexfen's reader and friend Burl Lampert.

on every take. "She looked drunk--who cared?" he said. Also, Lon Chaney unable to function after lunch (read: smashed).

Reading was always our bedrock; I'd also read and re-read to him his favorite classics. His favorite author was [Frederick] Marryat, who wrote the novel *Mr. Midshipman Easy*. I loved reading it, adding character voices as I went. It *is* a great tale, and I can see its influence on Jack in everything he wrote. He first read that book as a seven-year-old in Mill Valley (where we went to school with the future Eve Arden), and quickly went through the rest of Marryat, and he followed with all the adventure classics. Oy!, did he light up when I read those books. We both had so much fun rediscovering them all. He had many sets of first editions...Jules Verne, Dickens. *But—*

As I said his eyesight was failing when we met. Lee said it was the great tragedy of his later life—he so loved to read, much more than writing. When I joined him, he was near the end of a series of medical procedures that he was certain would restore his sight. And he had gadgets galore...lighted magnifying mirrors, magnifying glasses. Oh, it was so depressing, because obviously nothing worked. I came into the house one day and was talking with Lee downstairs, and there were these thumps that kept coming from upstairs, from Jack's office. Lee said that he had forbad her entry, and wanted to be left alone. Naturally I went right up... and it was one of the saddest things I ever saw: Jack, in his wheelchair, had pulled down piles of his books (remember those first editions?) and was tearing the books apart, sobbing, and with amazing strength. He'd grab a book, open it, hold it up to his eyes and try to force the vision to happen...and yank! Yank! He'd pull off a cover, tear a binding, and throw the book down. When I got there that day, he was sitting amid about 100 books. I stood there until he noticed me, and I just said, quietly, "Oh...Jack...I'm so sorry." I waded through the piles of pages and glue and book covers, and sort of leaned on his desk, and I put my arm around him, and hung my head with his. Now this was a very proud, unintentionally homophobic man, but he wept very quietly, and we sat there for a long time. Then he just sat up, wiped his nose on his kimono (his standard working wardrobe), extended that bony old arm, and said, "Okay, Burl. What are we working on?" That scenario was repeated two or three more times, in a smaller degree, over a few more months, and then he

"Jack loved sailing, he loved being on the water," Lampert recalled. "He sort of 'needed' to be around water. In the later years, he'd spend time on the deck of his house: He could see the Bay well enough, and all the plants surrounding him made him feel he was on an island."

somehow came to terms with his situation. He really never recovered from that, but he kept going, always determined to sell one last script.

Jack had one leg amputated below the knee in '99 and in the last 18 months that I was with him, he became bedridden. He loved nothing more than being propped up in bed, the TV brought to a few inches from him--there he could just barely see the images. He'd watch his own films, but usually just one per day. He also loved to watch Judy Garland. He was crazy for her. His story of chasing her around the MGM lot was priceless. I told him he was among the elite: a straight man who loved Judy Garland. He made a sour face and gave me a lecture: He said "the double-gaiters" [gays and bisexuals] just had an extra gene of good taste! *Everyone* loved her, he reminded me many times. I got tapes of her films and TV shows, and he loved all of it.

I would usually put on a tape of a Judy Garland concert episode for him to watch when I left for the day.

Jack actually preferred to think of himself as a newspaperman…a much more respectable occupation than moviemaking. Naturally his favorite play was *The Front Page*. In 2001 I was cast in a production of *The Front Page* at the Altarena Theatre in Alameda. I had two juicy parts. The Altarena is in the round, seats rising all around like a coliseum, and the way the seats were arranged, we had no spot for his wheelchair. So we put him on the stage, right next to a battered piano. And we worked his name into the script several times. I never, never saw him so happy! He and Lee attended all my shows, but this one was the topper. Being able to do that for Jack was one of the single best things I've ever done, I think.

Those six years with him were some of the best in my life. Jack changed my life in many ways, almost all for the better. He and Lee opened up new worlds to me.

INDESTRUCTIBLE MAN: Notes on the Script

By Tom Weaver

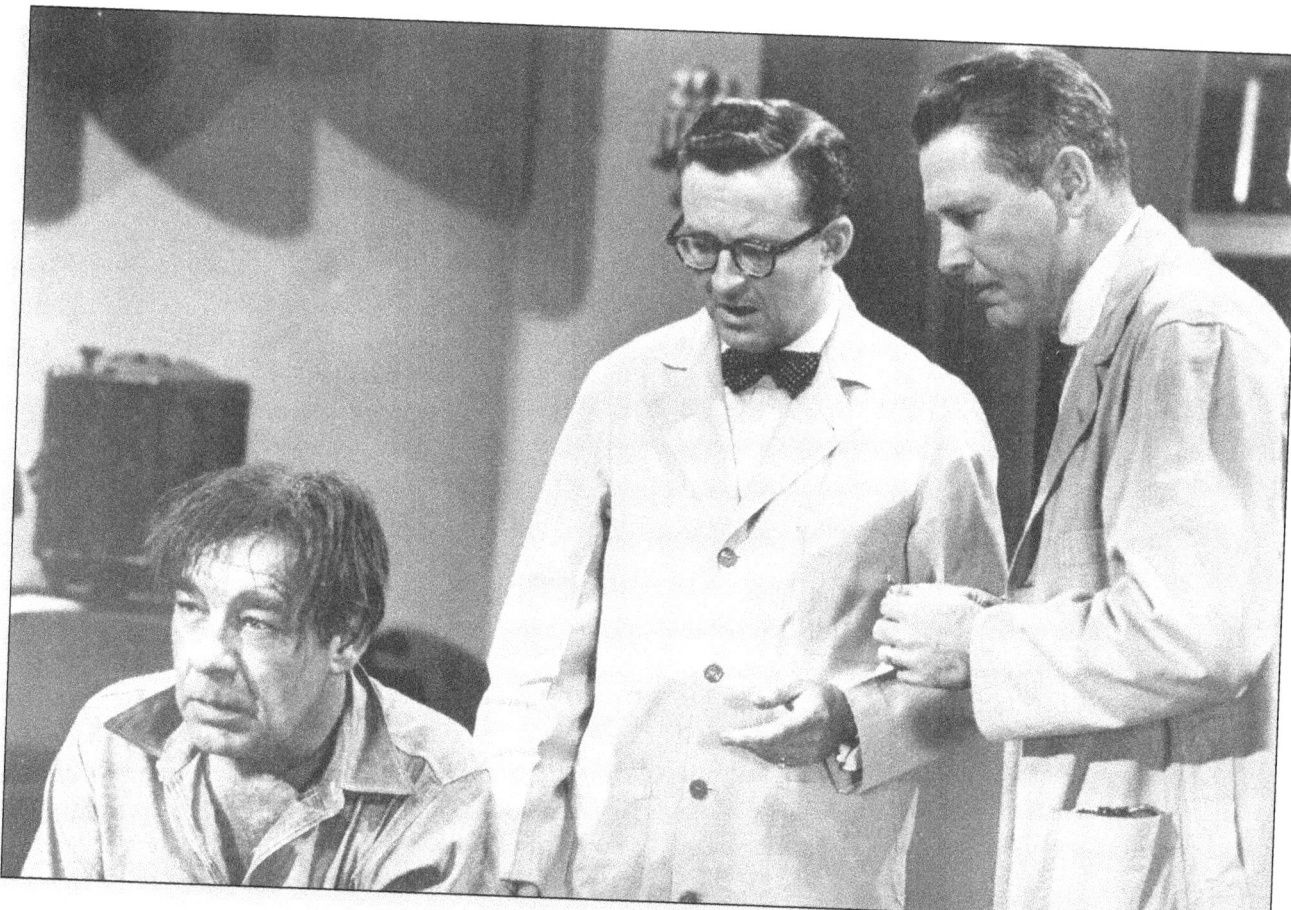

The lab set may be low-rent but Chaney's resurrection scene is one of the best in the picture, with giant closeups of his face and hand combining with the bombastic music to create a sense of great power in the awakening-from-the-dead man. (Pictured: Chaney, Joe Flynn, Robert Shayne.)

This is a by-no-means-complete list of some of the interesting (or funny, or bizarre) ways in which the script and the finished film differ.

⚡ The title on the cover of the script is *The Indestructible Man* but the article didn't make it to the screen.

⚡ Paul Lowe, Squeamy Ellis and Joe Marcelli are introduced in a pre-credits sequence on pages 1 and 2. Also on page 1, we learn from the narrator that Benton is about to be executed for the "brutal murders" of the armored car's guard and driver, a detail not included in the movie, where we get the impression that California imposes the death penalty on armored car robbers!

⚡ In the movie, Eva maintains that she was never Benton's girlfriend and was not aware that he was a criminal. This script features an Eva who laughs bitterly at herself as she exclaims, "Call me dumb… I didn't even—know—he was mixed up—in the rackets!," but never says anything to dispel the impression that she *was* his girl. On the day of Benton's execution, this script's Eva takes it a lot harder than the movie Eva: This script's Eva delivers one line with mounting hysteria and "buries her face in her hands, her shoulders shaking with sobs" (page 3). Later, after she does her stage act, she's still crying (pages 5 and 6).

⚡ In this script, Benton makes his first appearance as a thickly blanketed corpse on a wheeled stretcher in the underground electrical control room of a power installation on the outskirts of San Francisco. The script provides Dr. Bradshaw with the first name James and describes him as youngish, and he has lines like "He's a beauty" (referring to Benton's corpse); this gives the reader a mental image of an actor very different from Robert Shayne in the role. The script describes his assistant as "a big man" but milquetoast Joe Flynn landed that role in the movie.

⚡ As Bradshaw examines the Butcher's body (page 10), "[h]e indicates a metal plate" and says, "I may be prejudiced, but it isn't every day we get hold of a nice fresh one—even one with a plate in his head." I don't know how Bradshaw is able to determine, from eyeballing Benton's body, that he has a plate in his head. On page 12, as Bradshaw adjusts a fluoroscope plate over the body,

> the metal plate in the head starts to glow. (It will throughout the story when the Indestructible Man is in a state of rage or tension.)

If this had been done, *Indestructible Man would* have been highly reminiscent of Chaney's first Universal Horror, *Man Made Monster*.

⚡ The movie gives us our first indications of the strength of the reanimated Benton when he kayoes Bradshaw with an awkward southpaw shove and then knocks a door off its hinges with a tap from one shoulder. The power of the Indestructible Man is better showcased by the action described in this script (page 15): Just by brushing Bradshaw with a non-violent gesture, Benton sends the scientist spinning away "as though shot out of a cannon." As Benton shakes the doorknob of the battery room, it comes off in his hand, and when he squeezes it, it squashes as though it was clay. The script has him kill Bradshaw and the assistant one at a time (pages 20 and 21) rather than simultaneously as seen in the movie.

⚡ The feat of lifting Carney's Olds makes Benton rather pleased with himself, and at one point he holds it up with one hand (page 31).

⚡ Unexpurgated Man: "Butcher" Benton has no dialogue in the movie post-gas chamber but the script did give the reanimated Benton some lines: Look for them on script pages 30, 31, 32, 41-44, 58, 81 and 84-85. The script describes the way he talks as thick and slurred, "like that of a man who has recently suffered a stroke (page 17). At first he talks Tarzan-like (or, if you prefer, Frankenstein Monster-like), with lines to Carney like "Tire's flat…" and "Change—tire—" but soon begins speaking more normally.

⚡ The Lt. Chasen of the movie must be a bit less prosperous than the one in this script: In the movie, he tempts Eva with the promise of a hamburger. In this script, he dangles the prospect of a steak sandwich (page 29).

⚡ In the carjacking scene in the movie, Carney's girl is a pretty brunette who never says a word or makes a sound. In the script, she's a blonde who speaks at the beginning and the end of the scene. She's obviously turned on by the way Benton lifts the Olds and, after the tire's been changed, flirts with him: "You were real sweet, Muscleboy, stopping just because of me. I'd like to know you better." Benton kills Carney by lifting him overhead and throwing him out into the darkness, and puts an end to the blonde's screaming via a slap in the face that sends her reeling. Probably the reason Benton does *not* slap the girl in the movie: In the PCA letter to Pollexfen, censor Geoffrey Shurlock wrote, "In an

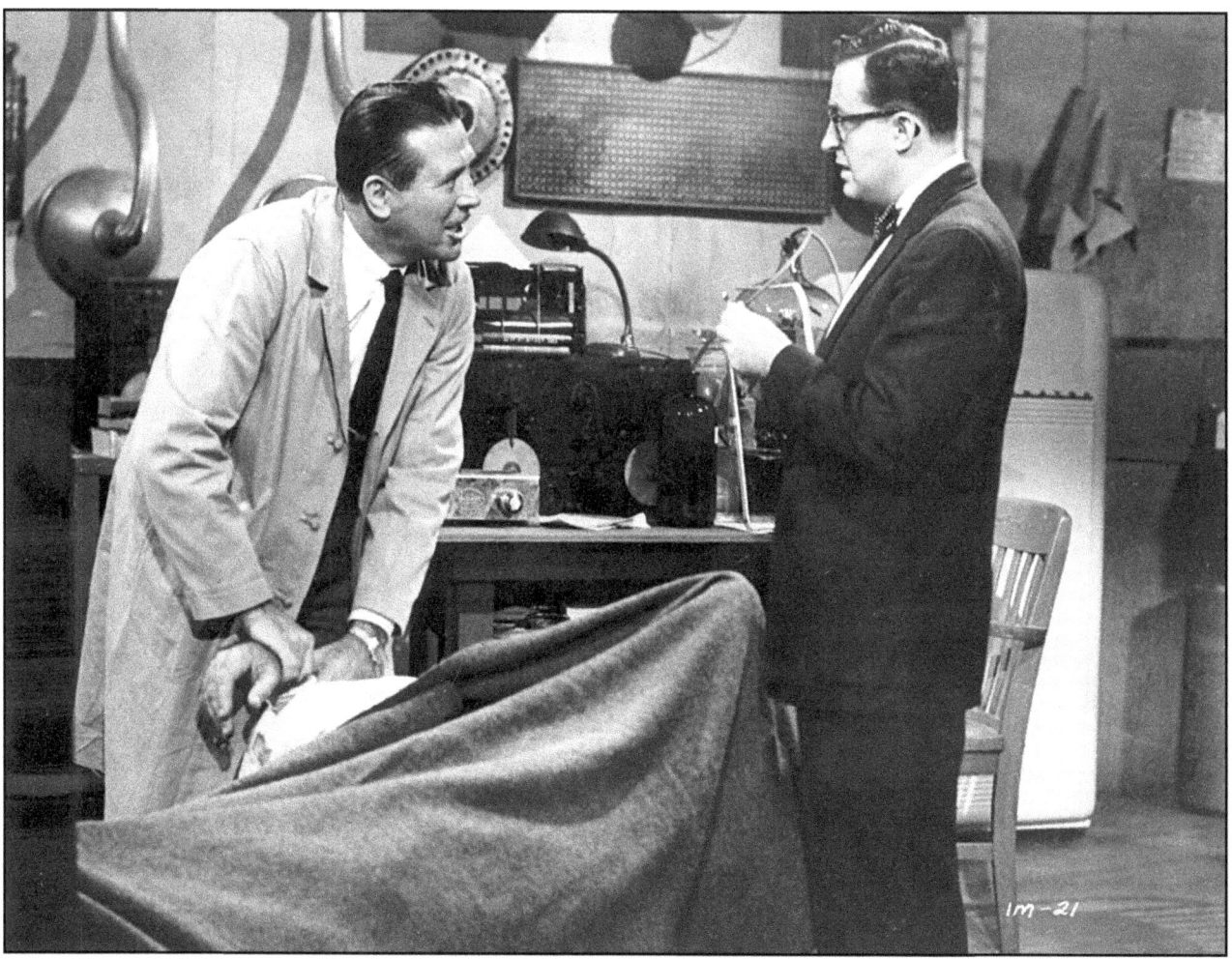

Cancer researcher Dr. Bradshaw and his assistant prepare to give the body of "Butcher" Benton a 287,000-volt charge. Well, that's one way to cure cancer! (Pictured: Robert Shayne, Joe Flynn.)

effort to avoid any excessive brutality, we ask that you eliminate the brutalizing of the blonde."

◆ In a gratuitous bit of mayhem, motorist Benton is on hand when a dump truck crashes on a dirt road and bursts into flames. The driver is trapped in the cab. As an old lady motorist watches, Benton approaches the flaming truck, assesses the situation, finds a spot he can grab onto—and drags the truck to the edge of a drop-off, and then pushes it over!

◆ Pages 35-38: Dave and Bert, cops in a patrol car, see the stolen Olds pass, give chase and shoot out a tire. Benton tries to escape on foot but the cops fire at him, hitting him three times. When Benton realizes that the bullets aren't hurting him, he U-turns and goes after the cops, "a look of fiendish triumph on his face." After he dispatches them, the fact of his new invulnerability hits him and he throws back his head laughing.

◆ In this script, Benton's stolen $600,000, *and* the armored car, are under 20 feet of water in a sump pit north of San Fernando Valley. Beginning at this point, page 70 of the 91-page script, this script and the finished film become almost completely different. Read my synopsis of these last 22 pages on pages 21-22 or, better yet, read those 22 pages for yourself.

Final Draft
11/4/54

"THE INDESTRUCTIBLE MAN"

by

Vy Russell

and

Sue Bradford

Property of:

JACK POLLEXFEN PRODUCTIONS, INC.
Jerry Fairbanks Studios
6052 Sunset Boulevard
Hollywood 28, California

HOllywood 2-1101

POLLEXFEN - RUSSELL - BRADFORD

"THE INDESTRUCTIBLE MAN"

FADE IN:

1   EXT. SAN QUENTIN - DAY (STOCK)

Narration over.

>   NARRATION
> San Quentin prison - the 17th
> of November. At five p.m.
> Charles - the Butcher - Benton
> would die here, payment for the
> brutal murders of guard and
> driver in a $600,000 armored
> car holdup in Los Angeles.
> Three people would breathe
> easier after the execution --

                                            START DISSOLVING TO:

2   EXT. STREET - DAY - CLOSE ESTABLISHING SHOT - PAUL LOWE

walking along street - shot for identification.

>   NARRATION
>   (continuing)
> For these three the Butcher had
> sworn to kill - somehow, some
> way -- Paul Lowe, his lawyer who
> had double-crossed him...

                                              WIPE TO:

3   INT. BAR - DAY - ESTABLISHING SHOT

SQUEAMY ELLIS, a wizened, rat-faced man, and JOE MARCELLI, a cripple, sit together at the end of the bar. Joe's crutches are propped beside him. Each man has a drink in front of him.

4   CLOSE SHOT - SQUEAMY

>   NARRATION
> Squeamy Ellis, a small-time
> fence - he tipped off the
> police....

2.

5   CLOSE SHOT - JOE

                    NARRATION
          Joe Marcelli. Tough. Joe had
          turned State's witness under
          pressure from Paul Lowe.

                                        DISSOLVE TO:

6   MAIN TITLES, CREDITS

                                        DISSOLVE TO:

7   EXT. MAIN STREET BURLESQUE HOUSE - DAY - ESTABLISHING SHOT

    DICK CHASEN stands looking at a life-size cardboard cutout
    of Eva Martin in scanty costume - seductively posed. Two
    notices pasted on the cutout read: L.A.'S HEAT WAVE CON-
    TINUES. MISS EVA MARTIN.

                    NARRATION
          In fifteen minutes, the Butcher
          would die. I decided to visit
          his girl friend, Eva Martin.

8   CLOSE SHOT - FAVORING CUTOUT

                    NARRATION
          I'm Dick Chasen, L.A. Police.

9   CLOSE SHOT - CHASEN

    checking watch. He starts out of shot heading for stage
    door alleyway.

                                        WIPE TO:

10 INT. DRESSING ROOM - ESTABLISHING SHOT - EVA

    The room contains a mirrored dressing table, a cupboard, a
    dressing screen, a wardrobe rack with a shelf above it. A
    picture of Butcher on dressing table. EVA is looking at
    the picture as a knock SOUNDS on the door.

                    EVA
          Come in---

    The door opens and Chasen enters. Eva turns, recognizes
    him.

                    EVA (cont'd)
          Oh. What do you want?

                                        (CONTINUED)

10   CONTINUED: (1)

Chasen closes the door behind him.

> CHASEN
> I'd like to talk to you...

Eva reacts. She's nervous - uncertain - not too friendly.

> EVA
> (shrugging)
> Talk -- you're a cop, aren't you?

Chasen sighs, sits on a chair by the door.

> CHASEN
> (wryly)
> That's a good question. It's been a year now and I haven't found the $600,000 or the three-ton armored car!

Eva reacts - her temper flaring.

> EVA
> I've told you and I've told you - I don't know where it is - I never did---

She stops, fighting for control.

> CHASEN
> Benton's going to be dead in a little while. I thought it might make a difference.

> EVA
> (with mounting hysteria)
> I never knew anything - call me dumb...
> (laughing bitterly at herself)
> I didn't even - know - he was mixed up - in the rackets!

She buries her face in her hands, her shoulders shaking with sobs. Chasen comes to his feet - unsure - his normal cynicism faltering - then he moves to her, puts his arms around her.

> CHASEN
> All right, kid - take it easy -

> VOICE (o.s.)
> You're on, Eva.

(CONTINUED)

4.

10   CONTINUED: (2)

Eva turns away - exits. Chasen goes out after her.

                                                    WIPE TO:

11   EXT. STAGE DOOR ALLEYWAY - ESTABLISHING SHOT

The shoeshine boy dozes in customer's seat, newspaper over face. A sign, lettered FOLLIES BURLESQUE - STAGE ENTRANCE - NO ADMITTANCE, is on wall across from him. Chasen comes down the alley toward CAMERA, passes shoeshine stand, would turn and go on CAMERA LEFT, but he sees:

12   MED. LONG SHOT - P.O.V. - PAUL LOWE

Lowe is just turning away from cardboard cutout toward the stage door alleyway.

                    NARRATION
           Paul Lowe - he was interested
           in that money -- interested
           too, in Eva...I decided to
           play a hunch---

13   MED. SHOT

TO ESTABLISH Chasen stepping up to sit on seat beside shoeshine boy, picks up newspaper off boy's face to hold in front of his face. Lowe comes into shot, turns into alleyway and continues along it. Chasen looks after him over newspaper.

                                                    WIPE TO:

14   INT. HALLWAY BACKSTAGE - ESTABLISHING SHOT

Paul is just coming down the hall. SOUND: music from o.s. stage. Paul looks at clock.

15   INSERT - CLOCK

hands of which stand at 4:50.

16   INT. THEATRE LONG SHOT (STOCK) - STAGE SHOW

The performers are not identifiable.

17   MED. SHOT - TIGHT ANGLE FROM WINGS - EVA, ON STAGE

CUT AWAY as Eva begins drastic strip action.
                                                    DISSOLVE TO:

5.

18 INSERT - CLOCK

on bar shows 5:05...The radio is carrying a news broadcast.

19 INT. BAR - DAY - MED. SHOT

Squeamy and Joe are intent on the radio.

> RADIO ANNOUNCER
> ---a few moments ago, Butcher
> Benton, without revealing the
> whereabouts of the $600,000
> stolen in the armored car
> holdup, paid for his crimes
> against society in the gas
> chamber at San Quentin.....
> Now for a look at the
> international scene. Today---

Squeamy and Joe both down their drinks - look at each other - relieved - the moment the Announcer finishes the line about Butcher.

CUT TO:

20 MED. SHOT - HALLWAY BACKSTAGE

Paul has stepped into the doorway of Eva's dressing room as the SOUND of the finale music up and finishing, followed by the SOUND of very scattered applause, comes over. Eva hurries into shot from direction of stage, pulling the robe around her and carrying her costume. Her face is anxious, unhappy. As she reaches Paul, the SOUNDS of music and applause have died and the SOUND of the radio from her dressing room can be heard. Eva goes on in, Paul following.

21 INT. EVA'S DRESSING ROOM - ESTABLISHING SHOT

Paul over to switch off radio.

> RADIO ANNOUNCER
> ....what went on in the United
> Nations Council---

Paul switches off radio, then pats Eva's shoulder comfortingly - enjoying his proximity.

> PAUL
> Come on, baby. Don't waste
> tears on Benton.

Eva pulls slightly away from him, looks at him squarely as she brushes away her tears. Eva has the suggestion of a lisp in her voice.

(CONTINUED)

21   CONTINUED: (1)

> EVA
> (hurt, puzzled)
> I feel so sorry for Charles.
> Maybe I could have done
> something - if I had known...

Paul nearly snorts with impatience but forces himself to be gentle with Eva.

> PAUL
> (cheerfully)
> How about a drink? We could
> both use one.

> EVA
> (rather shocked,
> reprovingly)
> An artist can't drink when
> she's working, Paul.

> PAUL
> (wryly)
> Oh...

Eva has remembered something. She goes to wardrobe rack, on tiptoe, reaches up to shelf, trying to find something. Paul watches for a moment, then:

> PAUL (cont'd)
> Can I help---?

> EVA
> (still searching)
> No ---
> (her hand has
> found an en-
> velope)
> I've found it...

Eva turns back toward Paul, looking down at envelope. Her face puckers up, quietly she begins to cry again.

> PAUL
> (coming to her,
> concerned)
> What is it, Eva? What's the
> matter now?

> EVA
> (trying to control
> her tears, indi-
> cating envelope)
> It's a message from Charles ---
> He - told me to read it - if he
> - died...

(CONTINUED)

21   CONTINUED: (2)

Paul's expression becomes shrewd, calculating - he automatically starts to reach for the envelope as o.s. SOUND of knock on door interrupts, and a nasal voice calls out:

                    VOICE (o.s.)
          Finale, Eva...!

                    EVA
              (calling back
               automatically)
          All right---

Eva reacts instinctively, picks up headdress and starts out, leaving envelope on dressing table.

                    PAUL
              (watching her)
          How about a steak after the
          show?

                    EVA
              (dispiritedly)
          Not tonight, Paul. Thanks.

Her face is still sad, but her rear swishes in the classical strut as she crosses room and exits. Paul waits until the door is closed after her, then grabs the envelope, opens it and extracts a sheet of paper from it. He reads rapidly, his lips curving in a wide, satisified smile. He starts to pocket the note, thinks better of it, holds it over an ashtray and deliberately burns it. Then he takes a fifty dollar bill from his wallet, puts it in the envelope and reseals it, lays it on the dressing table and exits.

                                        DISSOLVE TO:

22   EXT. SAN FRANCISCO POWER INSTALLATION - DAY - ESTABLISHING SHOT

                    NARRATION
          400 miles north, on the outskirts
          of San Francisco....

23   INT. UNDERGROUND ELECTRICAL CONTROL ROOM - DAY - ESTABLISHING SHOT

DR. JAMES BRADSHAW, youngish, intelligent, enters, closing door behind him. He checks various meters, dials, etc. He carries a notebook and refers to it in his checking. He also glances at his watch.

                                        (CONTINUED)

23   CONTINUED:

                    NARRATION
          ...another person was concerned
          with the Butcher's death - for
          Dr. James Bradshaw, distinguished
          biochemist, was making final
          preparations for an experiment -

     Bradshaw goes to door of battery storage room.

                    NARRATION (cont'd)
          Bradshaw impatiently awaited
          the arrival of his assistant --

     CAMERA PANS Bradshaw into:

24   INT. BATTERY STORAGE ROOM - ESTABLISHING SHOT

     Bradshaw takes a quick look around.

                    NARRATION
          In the next few hours, he hoped
          to repeat his success with
          laboratory animals on a human
          body....

     Bradshaw glances at watch again. CAMERA PANS him out of
     door.

25   INT. STAIRWAY - SHOOTING UP - ESTABLISHING SHOT

     as Bradshaw goes up the stairs on the double.

                                                  WIPE TO:

26   INT. LAB - ESTABLISHING SHOT

     A large metallic box is built into one end of the room.
     On one of its sides are several meters, indicating voltage,
     etc., and a master switch lever. The room is also equipped
     with a fluoroscope machine, powerful microscope, tray of
     surgical tools, transfusing equipment, small compressor,
     temperature controlled cabinet, and a centrifuge. A shelf
     is lined with specimen jars. Bradshaw comes in from stair-
     way door - moves about checking the various pieces of
     equipment.

                                              (CONTINUED)

26   CONTINUED:

> NARRATION
> ...and lead the way to a cure for cancer. Cancer cells have the ability to multiply at an enormous rate. Bradshaw reasoned that if he could duplicate such activity - change the mollecular structure itself - he would be on the road to learning control of it. Atoms could be split - why not life cells, whose reproductive processes depended on the same principle....?

27   CLOSE SHOT - BRADSHAW AT ELECTRICAL DIALS

> NARRATION
> Of prime importance to his experiment was electrical shock - of tremendous voltage....

Bradshaw to window.

28   P.O.V. - POWER INSTALLATION - STATION WAGON

LAP DISSOLVE TO:

29   INT. LAB - MED. SHOT

as the SOUND of knock on door comes over. Bradshaw goes to door, opens it. A big man, Bradshaw's ASSISTANT, stands beside a wheeled stretcher on which lies a thickly blanketed figure. Bradshaw helps roll the stretcher into the lab and over alongside the transfusing equipment.

> BRADSHAW
> You made good time.

> ASSISTANT
> (grinning)
> I didn't waste any.

> BRADSHAW
> Any trouble?

> ASSISTANT
> (shakes head)
> I handed over the money, moved the body into your station wagon, and that was that.

30 MED. CLOSE SHOT

   The Assistant removes a large bottle of dark-colored liquid from a temperature-controlled cabinet. Bradshaw gets a syringe and needle from surgical tray. The Assistant puts the bottle on table, Bradshaw throws the blanket off body.

   BRADSHAW
   He's a beauty.

   Bradshaw takes one arm of body and inserts needle in vein to extract a small amount of blood. Assistant glances at body.

   ASSISTANT
   (dubiously)
   Well - maybe...but did you notice this---?

   He indicates a metal plate.

   BRADSHAW
   (grins)
   ...I may be prejudiced, but it isn't every day we get hold of a nice fresh one -- even with a plate in his head....

   Bradshaw finishes drawing off blood, turns to table with microscope equipment. He puts a drop of the blood from the syringe on a slide, places the slide in the microscope - looks into it, adjusting the focus, steps back to let the Assistant look.

31 INSERT - MICROSCOPE FIELD

   SHOWING the blood cells - inert.

32 MED. CLOSE SHOT - BRADSHAW AND ASSISTANT

   Bradshaw takes the syringe, draws some of the dark fluid from the bottle into it - places it in the centrifuge a moment - then puts a drop of that mixture on slide, places the slide in microscope. He looks, exclaims - pleased.

33 INSERT - MICROSCOPE FIELD

   SHOWING blood cells - active now, multiplying with great rapidity - filling the field with an almost solid mass.

34 MED. CLOSE TWO SHOT

   as Assistant takes a quick look, nods approvingly at
   (CONTINUED)

34 CONTINUED:

Bradshaw. Both men turn back to the body on the stretcher. The Assistant takes the large bottle of dark fluid, installs it upside down in the cage receptacle of the transfusing equipment. Bradshaw has been inserting the transfusing needle into an arm; now he tapes the needle and tube securely.

                    BRADSHAW
          Start the compressor....

Assistant starts a small motor operating. The liquid in the bottle begins to go down. Quickly, Bradshaw and Assistant secure a flat-pronged wire around edge of stretcher, then Assistant moves to metallic box, opens door, revealing bevelled rim inside at proper level for contact with stretcher.

35 CLOSE SHOT - FULL BOTTLE

                                        FAST DISSOLVE TO:

36 CLOSE SHOT - BOTTLE

almost empty. CAMERA PULLS BACK as Bradshaw, standing by bottle, disconnects it as last of fluid empties out, removes tube from arm of corpse, and wheels stretcher over and into box. Assistant closes, fastens door of box. Bradshaw is now over by controls.

                    BRADSHAW
          Ready?

Assistant steps hurriedly back from box as he nods - joins Bradshaw at controls. Bradshaw swings lever. SOUND of ominous hum, rising in pitch.

37 INSERT - DIALS

as needle swings - indicating voltage: 287,000 volts.

38 *MONTAGE - ELECTRICAL STUFF INSIDE AND OUTSIDE

linked by SOUND, ending with:

                    ASSISTANT
                   (impressed)
          Two hundred and eighty-seven
          thousand volts!

                                        (CONTINUED)

38 CONTINUED:

> BRADSHAW
> (watching dials)
> Get the fluorscope set. We'll
> check with that before we start
> dissecting.

Assistant goes to fluorscope, loosens ratchet, adjusts to desired height, parallel to floor. Bradshaw waits a second longer, then swings switch lever to "off." SOUND of hum diminishes, dies.

> BRADSHAW (cont'd)
> That's it.

He slips on an asbestos glove, unbolts box door and opens it, rolls stretcher out and over beside fluorscope machine.

39 MED. CLOSE SHOT - BRADSHAW, ASSISTANT, BODY

Bradshaw pats the body.

> BRADSHAW
> Now, old chap, if you've
> responded properly and my
> figuring is right, you'll
> be more famous dead than
> alive.

He adjusts fluorscope plate over the body....As he does, the metal plate in the head starts to glow. (It will throughout the story when the Indestructible Man is in a state of rage or tension.)

> BRADSHAW (cont'd)
> All right - switch off the
> lights.

40 INSERT - FLUOROSCOPIC SHOT

as the plate moves slowly over head, throat, along an arm, back, and over chest cavity.

> ASSISTANT (o.s.)
> Wait!

The plate stops.

> ASSISTANT (o.s. cont'd)
> (puzzled)
> I thought I saw a pulsation....

The plate moves back to heart area. There is no movement for a moment, then a slight contraction of the heart muscle.

(CONTINUED)

40   CONTINUED:

                    BRADSHAW (o.s.)
                You're right!

Again the heart contracts, expands and again...

                    ASSISTANT (o.s.)
                  (incredulous)
                Dr. Bradshaw - his heart's
                beginning to beat! You've
                brought this man back to life!

                    BRADSHAW (o.s.)
                  (with certainty)
                No. The heart muscle has
                responded to terrific electrical
                shock. That's all.
                  (pleased)
                But it does prove that the cells
                still function. Turn on the
                lights...

41   MED. SHOT

        as the lights turn on. Bradshaw switches off fluorscope, moves it away from body.

                    BRADSHAW
                Get the instruments ready---

        Bradshaw goes over to microscope, selects some slides, etc. Assistant goes to surgical tray, turns to wheel it back, stops short as he sees the Butcher:

42   CLOSE SHOT - BUTCHER

        He suddenly stiffens, his back arches convulsively. CAMERA PULLS BACK to:

43   MED. SHOT - ASSISTANT IN F.G.

                    ASSISTANT
                  (tense)
                Dr. Bradshaw!

        Bradshaw turns, puzzled by Assistant's tone; his gaze switches to Butcher at SOUND of loud groan from Butcher.

        CAMERA PANS both men as they hurry to Butcher's side. BUTCHER IN F.G. Suddenly the Butcher's eyes open, but they are glazed, unseeing.

                                                (CONTINUED)

43   CONTINUED: (1)

                    ASSISTANT (cont'd)
                (shaken)
            He _is_ alive...

                    BRADSHAW
                (trying to figure)
            A shock reaction...It can't
            last --

                    ASSISTANT
                (with meaning)
            Cells are multiplying now if
            your theory is right...

                    BRADSHAW
                (nodding)
            If only we _could_ keep this
            reaction going longer...It's
            worth a try.
                (urgent)
            Get some adrenalin from the
            supply room - aminophyline,
            too....Hurry!

Assistant exits, Bradshaw literally shoving him out door.
Butcher groans again. Bradshaw hurries to his side. He
passes his hand in front of Butcher's eyes. They remain
glassy, unseeing. Bradshaw snaps his fingers sharply, but
there is no reaction. He reaches for Butcher's wrist to
check his pulse. Suddenly Butcher's arm reaches out,
squeezes around Bradshaw convulsively. Bradshaw struggles
helplessly, unable to get away....As suddenly, Butcher's
arm drops back on stretcher, limp -- Bradshaw steps quickly beyond his reach, feels his side gingerly, lets out a
heartfelt sigh of relief....He watches Butcher a moment
with new respect, suspicion -- then hurries to medicine
cabinet, searches, selects a vial, reacts, turns back at
SOUND of stretcher creaking - Butcher is struggling to
sit up.

                    BRADSHAW (cont'd)
                (instantly)
            Hey...!

He deliberately controls his voice, speaks soothingly but
commandingly:

                    BRADSHAW (cont'd)
            Lie still. Your heart can't
            stand the strain....

Butcher's head turns in Bradshaw's direction as he speaks,
but his eyes are still unseeing. Butcher is now sitting
up; Bradshaw approaches him cautiously...

                                              (CONTINUED)

43   CONTINUED: (2)

                          BRADSHAW (cont'd)
                        (firmly)
                    You must lie down...

Bradshaw reaches Butcher, hesitates, then places hand on
shoulder to ease him back down. Butcher's head follows
SOUND of Bradshaw's voice, but eyes are glazed.

                          BRADSHAW (cont'd)
                    Easy does it, easy...

With a ponderous motion that suggests tremendous strength,
Butcher brushes Bradshaw aside like a straw. The gesture
is not violent, but the results are. Bradshaw goes spinning back as though shot out of a cannon. SOUND of crashing shelves. The Butcher, groggy, gets to his feet. Instinctively, he searches for an exit, stumbles to the
nearest door which is closed. (This door leads to Battery
Room.)

44   MED. CLOSE SHOT - BUTCHER AT DOOR

He reaches to take the doorknob in his hand, examines it
and then gives it a shake - not exaggerated - but the doorknob comes free with a rending noise (SOUND). Butcher
looks down at the doorknob, puzzled.

45   INSERT - BUTCHER'S HAND, DOORKNOB

ESTABLISHING it in his hand. Butcher's fingers start closing around it, slowly, and the knob crumples in his hand
like it was clay instead of steel. The hand closes into a
fist and then opens - the knob is a lump of metal.

46   CLOSE SHOT - BUTCHER

reacting - looking at knob - his mind is not functioning
well enough to get the significance of this feat of
strength.

                          NARRATION
                    The Butcher had not only been
                    brought back to life - Bradshaw's
                    experiment to rearrange and
                    increase cellular structure had
                    given this creature enormous
                    strength....

47   MED. SHOT

Butcher tosses the hunk of metal, that was the doorknob,

                                              (CONTINUED)

47   CONTINUED:

aside, puts his hand on the door and pushes it open. He takes a couple of steps into the Battery Room, stops, looks around -fear showing on his face.

48   INT. BATTERY ROOM - ESTABLISHING SHOT

Butcher looking around, registering primitive, childlike fear - there is no exit from this room.

> NARRATION
> But the Butcher's brain was not yet functioning well enough for him to understand his strength - not yet capable of more than the simplest thought patterns and the most primitive instincts...

49   MED. SHOT

as the Butcher retreats from the Battery Room.

CUT TO:

50   INT. BRADSHAW LAB - MED. SHOT

Bradshaw is beginning to come to. He lies for a moment after his eyes open - taking it all in - remembering. Then, slowly, he gets up, wincing with pain as he does so. He starts for the telephone, reaches the instrument, lifts it, then hesitates. From o.s. the SOUND of Butcher's heavy footsteps are heard.

> NARRATION
> Bradshaw started to call the police, then changed his mind. He felt certain the Butcher's new lease on life was limited to a matter of minutes ---
> Scientific curiosity battled with caution and won. Bradshaw decided to handle the Butcher himself....

Bradshaw turns to face the door, the SOUND of Butcher's lumbering steps is coming nearer. Bradshaw stands, tense - waiting. The Butcher appears in the doorway, looks around the lab slowly - at Bradshaw - his expression puzzled, bewildered. Bradshaw stands quietly - aware of possible personal danger to himself, afraid yet eager.

(CONTINUED)

50   CONTINUED: (1)

> (NOTE: The Butcher always moves ponderously. When he speaks, his speech is thick, slurred - like that of a man who has recently suffered a stroke.)

BRADSHAW
Please sit down, Mr. Benton.
Let me help you.

Bradshaw takes jacket from hook. The Butcher stares at Bradshaw, then - his expression unchanged - he shambles over to chair indicated by Bradshaw and sits down. Bradshaw helps him put on jacket.

BRADSHAW (cont'd)
(approvingly)
Put this on - that's fine...

Bradshaw moves unhurriedly to cabinet drawer, takes out a stethoscope, but doesn't attempt to approach the Butcher yet. Butcher follows his every move.

BRADSHAW (cont'd)
Do you remember anything that
has happened?

Butcher doesn't answer. The two men stare at each other for a moment. Bradshaw's attention is caught by the o.s. SOUND of footsteps approaching. Butcher keeps his eyes glued on Bradshaw until Assistant bursts in, then switches his attention to Assistant briefly...Assistant takes in the situation, wonder and some fear on his face.

BRADSHAW (cont'd)
(softly, warningly)
Our 'beauty' plays rough---

Bradshaw moves over to Assistant, careful to make no hurried or startling movements. The Butcher watches openly. The two men watch him warily.

ASSISTANT
(impressed)
Boy - I'll say!

BRADSHAW
(nodding)
His strength is unbelievable!
Each cell must have multiplied
a hundred times - perhaps a
thousand...

Suddenly the Butcher's head drops back, he begins gasping for breath.

(CONTINUED)

50   CONTINUED: (2)

> BRADSHAW (cont'd)
> (speaking as he
> hurries to the
> Butcher; urgently)
> The aminophyline...

Assistant hands Bradshaw the cartridge which he breaks under Butcher's nose....The Butcher reacts, jerking his head back, then takes a deep, shuddering breath, beginning to revive. His eyes squint now, a degree of cunning and alertness in them.

> BUTCHER
> (thickly)
> Wha----?

> BRADSHAW
> Easy, Benton. Just relax.
> I'm a doctor----

Quickly, with some trepidation, Bradshaw starts to place stethoscope to Butcher's chest. Butcher pushes him away. Bradshaw goes reeling back. Assistant watches, horrified. Bradshaw nods to Assistant that he's all right - Bradshaw speaks to Butcher, his tone calm, reassuring, but he stays out of reach.

> BRADSHAW (cont'd)
> We want to try to help you...
> Do you understand me?

Butcher nods slowly, affirmatively.

> BUTCHER
> Where----?

> BRADSHAW
> You're in my laboratory - the
> execution was carried out and
> you were declared dead.

Butcher's brow wrinkles in a puzzled frown, he lifts his hands, looks at them - looks at the Assistant and Bradshaw, shakes his head.

> BUTCHER
> No----

(CONTINUED)

50   CONTINUED: (3)

                    BRADSHAW
                 (quickly)
            Yes - but I used your body for
            an experiment and brought you
            back to life - although I didn't
            intend that....Now, we want to
            take some blood samples - make
            some tests on you - find out
            what has happened.

Butcher starts coming to his feet. Bradshaw puts a restraining hand on his shoulder.

                    BRADSHAW (cont'd)
                 (soothingly)
            You've had a great shock - You
            must be quiet - we mean you no
            harm.

Butcher relaxes again. The Assistant, deciding all is well now, reaches for the syringe to draw a blood sample --- Butcher watches him closely as he approaches. Bradshaw takes the rubber tourniquet and applies it to Butcher's arm - talking reassuringly to Butcher as he does so.

                    BRADSHAW (cont'd)
            This won't hurt - it's just to
            make the vein stand ooout....

He has the tourniquet in place - holds the Butcher's arm in his hands - the Butcher is quiet but his eyes are watching every move of Bradshaw's and the Assistant's.

                    BRADSHAW (cont'd)
                 (to Assistant)
            Give me the syringe.

Assistant hands him the syringe, Bradshaw starts to put the needle in the vein.

51   INSERT - BUTCHER'S ARM, BRADSHAW'S HAND AND SYRINGE

     TO ESTABLISH the needle will not penetrate and as Bradshaw applies more pressure, the needle bends.

52   CLOSE THREE SHOT

     Bradshaw and Assistant look at each other.

                    ASSISTANT
                 (wonderingly)
            Why won't the needle penetrate?

                                                  (CONTINUED)

52 CONTINUED:

>   BRADSHAW
>   (slowly)
>   The tissue structure must be
>   a nearly solid mass of cells
>   now.
>
>   ASSISTANT
>   Will we be able to get the
>   blood samples?

Bradshaw is thinking - the two scientists are so engrossed in the clinical problem that neither of them is aware of the Butcher's growing apprehension. The Butcher's eyes have narrowed, his mouth twisted - his expression more alert.

>   BRADSHAW
>   Surgically perhaps.

53 MED. CLOSE THREE SHOT

Before the Assistant can answer this, Butcher comes to his feet, shaking Bradshaw's grip from his arm. Bradshaw is knocked down by the force of this slight movement.

>   BUTCHER
>   No!

Butcher starts to move away from the chair. Instinctively the Assistant reaches for him. Bradshaw is scrambling to his feet.

>   ASSISTANT
>   Hey --- wait...!

The Butcher turns on him, raises his arm, his fists clenched. The Assistant freezes with fear.

>   BRADSHAW
>   Run - run...!

But it's too late - the Butcher's upraised hands come down like two huge hammers on the Assistant and the man crumples to the floor. Butcher stands over him, looking down at him expressionlessly. Bradshaw rushes to kneel beside the Assistant, quickly examine him - then, horror on his face and in his voice, he looks up at the Butcher.

>   BRADSHAW (cont'd)
>   He's - dead...!

Butcher turns and starts moving toward the door leading outside. Bradshaw is frightened for his own safety but

(CONTINUED)

53   CONTINUED:

realizes this creature must not get away. He runs to the door, locks it, stands with his back against it. Butcher continues toward door.

> BRADSHAW (cont'd)
> (desperately)
> Benton - listen to me - you mustn't leave here...

Butcher moves on toward him - Bradshaw's words have no effect.

> BRADSHAW (cont'd)
> (frantic, voice rising)
> It isn't safe for you to leave! I'm responsible for you being alive - you must stay here so I can take care of you....

The Butcher has reached Bradshaw and without expression, he raises his arm - Bradshaw tries to duck away too late. Butcher hits him with a back hand sweep of his arm and Bradshaw is sent crashing against the wall and then to the floor where he lies quiet. Bradshaw's legs are in the way of the door, Butcher shoves them aside with his foot, takes hold of the door and shakes it gently - SOUND of the lock splintering and the door swings inward as we...

WIPE TO:

54   EXT. BRADSHAW'S LABORATORY - NIGHT - MED. SHOT

(COVER BUTCHER DURING CUT) TO ESTABLISH the Butcher coming out of the laboratory. The station wagon in which his body was delivered still stands outside. Butcher looks around, sees the station wagon, moves over to it.

> NARRATION
> Bradshaw was dead and the monster he had created was alive.....The Butcher's mind was not functioning normally yet - but some degree of memory - certain habit patterns - were reasserting themselves.

Butcher gets into the station wagon.

55   CLOSE SHOT - BUTCHER

as he scans the dashboard, moves the wheel with his hands - like a person trying to remember how to work a piece of

(CONTINUED)

22.

55 CONTINUED:

   machinery. He reaches for the keys - the ignition switch.
   He fumbles with the gear shift on the wheel - then the
   long familiar habits pay off - he gets the motor going
   with a roar. He gets the car in gear and starts off.

   WIPE TO:

56 EXT. HIGHWAY - NIGHT - ESTABLISHING SHOT - STATION WAGON
   RUN THROUGH

   ESTABLISHING the Butcher's erratic driving - the car is
   not going fast but is weaving from side to side.

57 INT. STATION WAGON - CLOSE SHOT - BUTCHER

   struggling to drive straight - his reactions are too slow.

   WIPE TO:

58 EXT. HIGHWAY - NIGHT - ANOTHER SPOT - STATION WAGON RUN
   THROUGH

   TO ESTABLISH the Butcher has the car under control now -
   he's still driving slowly but is staying on the right side
   of the road.

59 CLOSE SHOT - BUTCHER

   pleased with himself now.

   WIPE TO:

60 EXT. HIGHWAY CROSSROADS - NIGHT - ESTABLISHING SHOT -
   STATION WAGON

   Butcher pulls the station wagon to a stop beside the road
   signs, where headlights hit them.

61 INSERT - ROAD SIGN - HEADLIGHTS

   reading: LOS ANGELES 360 MILES.

                     NARRATION
           Los Angeles---

62 INT. CAR - CLOSE SHOT - BUTCHER

   digesting this. Frowning - then suddenly, his mouth sets

   (CONTINUED)

23.

62 CONTINUED:

grimly, purposefully - he puts the car in gear. Narration over:

> NARRATION
> ---those words meant something to the Butcher - Los Angeles - and three men he had sworn to kill...

DISSOLVE TO:

63 EXT. STORE FRONT - NIGHT - ESTABLISHING SHOT

Chasen is watching across street from bar.

> NARRATION
> I was sticking on the lawyer's tail back in L.A.....

64 ANOTHER ANGLE - CHASEN'S P.O.V. - BLUE HEAVEN BAR

Joe Marcelli is approaching the bar - he's drunk and his movements are clumsy, he's having difficulty maneuvering his crutches.

> NARRATION
> He'd had it parked in a cold saloon for a couple of hours before Joe Marcelli joined him. It looked more business than social to me.

CUT TO:

65 INT. BAR - NIGHT - MED. SHOT

Paul Lowe sits in a booth midway down the bar, facing the entrance. Almost opposite him, and closer to the door, a blowsy, DRUNKEN WOMAN sits on a bar stool. As Joe comes in, Paul alerts, looks at his watch - annoyed. Joe stops just inside the door, looks around, spots Paul and starts for him, swaying precariously on the crutches. The Woman has turned to look at him, she's already at the giggly stage and Joe strikes her funny.

> WOMAN LUSH
> (too loudly,
> to bartender)
> Hey - look at that! I seen 'em stagger on two legs but he's doin' it on four....

(CONTINUED)

65   CONTINUED: (1)

> Joe has nearly reached her. His face twists in an ugly grimace.

                JOE
       Shut up - you flea bag!

> The Woman's hilarity changes quickly to truculence.

             WOMAN LUSH
      Look who's callin' names --
      at least I'm no squealer --
      no stoolie!

> In spite of his drunkenness, Joe moves with surprising speed, brings one of his crutches up in a sweeping swing which would strike the Woman squarely, but the Bartender leans over the bar swiftly and grabs the crutch. Paul has moved in to group.

             BARTENDER
       (angrily, to Joe)
      I warned you before....

              PAUL
       (quickly, to
        Bartender)
      Never mind, I'll handle him.
      I want to talk to him.

> The Bartender hesitates a moment, then nods grudgingly.

             BARTENDER
      Okay, Mr. Lowe. But any future
      business you got with this
      psycho, take care of it in your
      office upstairs. He keeps
      showin' around here, sooner or
      later he's going to get slugged
      - cripple or no cripple.

              JOE
      Why - you....

              PAUL
       (to Joe)
      Shut up!

> Paul shoves Joe into the booth. There's a bottle and two shot glasses on the table. Joe reaches for the bottle but Paul pulls it over to his side as he sits down, keeps it in his hands.

              JOE
       (whining)
      I need a shot bad...

                              (CONTINUED)

65   CONTINUED: (2)

Paul looks around to make sure they can't be overheard.

>   PAUL
>   You'll get one - maybe. After
>   I finish talking to you. You
>   sober enough to understand?
>
>   JOE
>   (sullenly)
>   Yeah - I run out of dough.
>
>   PAUL
>   (stingingly)
>   No wonder - look at you - once
>   the best torch man in town --
>   now I doubt if you could crack
>   a safe if you knew the
>   combination.
>
>   JOE
>   (defensively)
>   No jobs - nobody wants me since
>   I turned State's on Benton.
>   That's your doing - you talked
>   me into it....
>
>   PAUL
>   (cutting in)
>   Stop crying. I have a job for
>   you - if you can stay off the
>   bottle....
>
>   JOE
>   (eagerly)
>   You know I can if I got a job.
>   How much - what is it?
>
>   PAUL
>   Two grand for you - we'll need
>   wrecking equipment - probably
>   be some underwater work...
>
>   JOE
>   (whispering)
>   You found the armored car ---
>   Where?
>
>   PAUL
>   (whispering)
>   Not far from where he pulled
>   the job - if it's still there.
>   Never mind that now - You
>   interested?

(CONTINUED)

65   CONTINUED: (3)

                    JOE
                (bargaining)
            Two grand isn't much - outta
            six hundred thousand....

                    PAUL
            There'll be other expenses --
            and the money's plenty hot --
            that's it - or do I get myself
            another boy?

                    JOE
                (quickly)
            All right - I'll do it....
            How soon do you----

                    PAUL
                (cutting in)
            Arrange it for tomorrow night
            - check with me before noon -
            I'm going to the races...

Joe reaches for bottle. Paul stops him.

                    PAUL (cont'd)
            One - and then no more until
            the job's done.

He lets Joe have the bottle.

                                        CUT TO:

66   EXT. ACROSS STREET FROM BAR - MED. SHOT - CHASEN IN F.G.

SAM with him....NARRATION OVER.

                    NARRATION
            I'd gotten an okay from the
            Captain to play along on my
            hunch. Sam arrived to take
            over. I briefed him, found
            I still had time to catch the
            last of Eva's show. Certain
            duties a cop doesn't resent
            doing on his own time.

Chasen out of shot.

                                        DISSOLVE TO:

67   INT. EVA'S DRESSING ROOM - NIGHT - MED. SHOT

    Eva is in dressing gown - her face is smeared with cold cream which she tissues off in rhythm with a "grind" which she is practicing very seriously, humming her own accompaniment tonelessly - SOUND of knock on door.

> EVA
> (spacing it, without interrupting routine)
>
> Come....in...

Chasen opens door, stands there smiling, watching Eva who is completely preoccupied figuring out this new variation -- Chasen applauds as she finishes.

> EVA (cont'd)
> (smiling at him)
>
> Hello --- Did you see the last show?

> CHASEN
>
> Part of it.

> EVA
> (repeating a couple of steps)
>
> This makes a better finish, don't you think so?

> CHASEN
> (grinning)
>
> I'd pay the price of admission to see it either way.

> EVA
> (pleased)
>
> Thanks...
> (quickly)
> No hard feelings, Chasen. You're just doing your job.

> CHASEN
> (a little uncomfortable)
>
> Yeah. Well.....

Eva flops down in front of dressing table, starts removing make-up again. Chasen takes chair beside door.

> CHASEN (cont'd)
> (as though changing subject)
>
> You figuring to stay on here, or what?

(CONTINUED)

67   CONTINUED: (1)

                    EVA
                (straight)
          I guess so...Vegas used to be
          a good town for us specialists,
          but all the movie stars are
          taking over the legitimate
          there now---

                    CHASEN
                (covering his
                 amusement)
          That so? ---
                (trying again)
          I wasn't thinking about work.
          Saw Paul Lowe coming in earlier.
          You two are pretty good friends,
          aren't you?

                    EVA
                (shrugs)
          No.

                    CHASEN
          Mind telling me what he wanted?

                    EVA
                (trying to remem-
                 ber, then shrug-
                 ging)
          He wanted to buy me a steak
          after the show.

Chasen rises.

                    CHASEN
                (grinning)
          So you already have a date?

                    EVA
          No....
                (very seriously)
          I don't go out with fellows
          much - they act so silly.

                    CHASEN
                (wryly)
          I was about to suggest I take
          you home---

                    EVA
                (seriously)
          That would be different. You're
          a cop.

                                      (CONTINUED)

67 CONTINUED: (2)

Chasen does a slight take.

> CHASEN
> (pretended warning)
> I'm off duty now.
> (quickly, laughing)
> How about a steak sandwich on the way?

> EVA
> (approving)
> Sounds nice...

Chasen starts to sit back down on the chair, but Eva, smoothly, sweetly and automatically, as if this is habit with her, opens the door, puts a gentle, guiding hand on his arm.

> EVA (cont'd)
> I won't be long---

And Chasen is through the door before he realizes it. She closes the door.

CUT TO:

68 INT. HALLWAY OUTSIDE DOOR - CLOSE SHOT - CHASEN

as he realizes how neatly he has been put out - looks at door, surprised -- then grins in appreciation, puts on hat, takes out a cigarette and leans against wall to wait.

FADE OUT:

FADE IN:

69 EXT. HIGHWAY - NIGHT - STATION WAGON

ESTABLISHING Butcher driving. Butcher holds the protesting car to a good clip. SOUND of rattling, wheezing car.

CUT TO:

70 SHOULDER OF HIGHWAY - NEW OLDS - ESTABLISHING SHOT

The Olds is pulled off to one side of highway, its lights still on. A shapely BLONDE stands revealed by headlights, waving for help at car approaching. SOUND: car going by. Girl gives come on - doesn't work. She reacts, then sees other car coming.

71	LONG SHOT - STATION WAGON, OLDS

as Butcher pulls past Olds, then suddenly comes to a squealing stop.

72	MED. SHOT

as Butcher gets out of car, goes back to Blonde.

> BLONDE
> (simpering)
> Gee, it's nice of you to stop
> to help me out....

Butcher pays her no attention - he's heading for the car. From the darkness beyond the Olds, CARNEY steps out.... Carney is short, fat, personable - a "spieler." Butcher stops short as he sees him, waiting to find out the score.

> CARNEY
> (spreading it on)
> Well, sir - you're a *real*
> gentleman - to be helping
> out strangers in distress...
> (laughs apolo-
> getically)
> Hope you don't mind me using
> the Babe there as a little
> bait - quite a dish, eh --
> that's what she gets paid for
> - bait, that is....She's a
> real shaker artist in my outfit.
> Carnival man, myself. Just call
> me Carney....

He sticks out hand for handshake - Butcher ignores it, and Carney hurries on:

> CARNEY (cont'd)
> Yeah. Well. We're in kind of
> a spot here. Flat tire. Brand-new
> car, and no tools in it. Some of
> these dealer's make our carnival
> grifters look like babes! Yeah.
> Well, now. If you'd just lend us
> a jack---

Butcher has started to walk around car. He stops at right front of car.

> BUTCHER
> (gruffly)
> Tire's flat...

Carney gives Butcher a quizzical look.

(CONTINUED)

72   CONTINUED:

                    CARNEY
          Yeah. Yeah.
               (to Blonde, rolling
                his eyes to indi-
                cate Butcher....
                purses his mouth
                wryly)
          Some gilhooley!
               (to Butcher)
          Yeah. Yeah. As I was saying,
          if you'd just lend----

73   MED. CLOSE SHOT - BUTCHER

     as he bends forward, starts to lift car up by bumper -
     using both hands - testing his strength, not sure he can
     do it. Then, with confidence, lifting front end of car.

74   MED. CLOSE SHOT - CARNEY

     his speech running down, eyes bugging out as he watches.

                    CARNEY
          ....us -- a ---- jack-----

     He's never nonplussed for long, but is thoroughly impressed

                    CARNEY (cont'd)
          Say. Look at that. Yeah,
          yeah....

75   ANOTHER ANGLE - INCLUDING BUTCHER AND CARNEY

     Butcher is rather pleased with himself. Now he tries hold-
     ing up car with one hand.

                    CARNEY
               (astonished,
                delighted)
          Say - who you signed up with?
          Whoever it is, he's not treating
          you right. Why, I could make a
          mint for both of us -- Think how
          the jaspers and thistlechins'd
          go for a act like that...
                    BUTCHER
               (interrupting, no
                longer interested
                in showing off)
          Change - tire ----

                                                  (CONTINUED)

75 CONTINUED:

                    CARNEY
                (doing take)
            Huh? --- With you holding up
            the car....?

                    BUTCHER
                (nastily)
            Now...!

                    CARNEY
                (nervously)
            Yeah. Yeah. Sure----

Carney shrugs a "get him" as he scurries to start changing tire.

                                        FAST DISSOLVE TO:

76 MED. SHOT - NIGHT

Carney is just finishing putting on hubcap. Butcher has started around car, Carney rises, brushing off hands.

                    CARNEY
                (really making
                  pitch)
            Sure wish you'd consider tying
            up with me, Mister----

Butcher continues toward driver's side of car. Blonde steps in front of him.

                    BLONDE
            You were real sweet, Muscleboy,
            stopping just because of me.
            I'd like to know you better.

Butcher has stopped, he looks right through Blondie as though she doesn't exist, then on past her toward driver's side, starts to get in, as:

                    BLONDE (cont'd)
                (getting it -
                  indignant)
            Hey! He wanted the car!

Carney rushes at Butcher - angry.

                    CARNEY
            Nobody's taking my car....!

Carney reaches Butcher, one fist waving. Butcher unemotionally lifts him up above his head, throws him off into

                                        (CONTINUED)

33.

76 CONTINUED:

darkness in direction of station wagon. The Blonde begins to scream piercingly, hystericaly. Butcher slaps her across face, she reels back into darkness, SOUND of small whimper. Butcher gets into car, starts it.

DISSOLVE TO:

77 EXT. HIGHWAY - NIGHT - RUN THROUGH

TO ESTABLISH Butcher passing truck.

DISSOLVE TO:

78 EXT. HIGHWAY - NIGHT - OLDS RUN THROUGH - DETOUR - DIRT ROAD

Butcher stops. The truck comes in fast, passes Butcher, turning onto dirt road detour. Butcher starts onto detour as truck goes out of sight around bend. O.S. SOUND: crash.

WIPE TO:

79 EXT. HIGHWAY - ESTABLISHING SHOT - WRECKED DUMP TRUCK, OLD CAR

A dump truck has skidded and crashed into the high bank after making a curve. The truck is on fire, the driver pinned in the cab. An old car has skidded to a stop nearby and its driver, a small, stringy WOMAN, has just gotten out. Butcher rounds the curve, sees the wreck blocking the road and slams on his brakes, skids into high bank - not damaging his car - and stops. Woman runs toward Butcher's car.

80 MED. CLOSE SHOT - OLDS

Butcher gets out of his car as Woman runs up to him. She grabs his arm, shouting and motioning frantically toward burning truck.

81 WIDE ANGLE SHOT

TO COVER the action of the Butcher. The flames are licking higher around the truck. Butcher walks over to it, looks the situation over briefly. Then, picking the easiest spot to get hold of the truck, he steps into it, grabs it, and swings it around, pushing it to the edge of the steep drop-off and over. SOUND: crash. ESTABLISH reaction of Woman who thought Butcher was going to try to rescue driver

(CONTINUED)

34.

81   CONTINUED:

and then her stunned reaction as Butcher pushes truck over drop-off.

Butcher looks over the drop-off for just a moment - turns - ignoring the Woman - and walks back to Olds, gets in, starts motor, backs it away from embankment, changes gear and drives away.

DISSOLVE TO:

82   EXT. CITY HALL - ESTABLISHING SHOT

83   INT. POLICE STATION - CLOSE SHOT - TELETYPE MACHINE

clicking away - bells ringing. Hand comes into shot as a message finishes, rips the paper from machine.

WIPE TO:

84   INT. LAUDER'S OFFICE DOOR - ESTABLISHING SHOT (OUTSIDE)

door lettered: "CAPTAIN J. I. LAUDER." as the DESK SERGEANT opens the door, goes in, carrying a piece of copy from a teletype machine.

WIPE TO:

85   INT. LAUDER'S OFFICE - MED. SHOT

LAUDER is using dictaphone, pauses to look at Desk Sergeant as he enters with bulletin.

                    DESK SERGEANT
Another All-Points from CHP.

Lauder reads bulletin.

                          LAUDER
                      (incredulously)
These reports sound like they
came from a batch of loonies---

                    DESK SERGEANT
                    (shrugs)
Sure do, but there it is....

DISSOLVE TO:

86 EXT. HIGHWAY - EARLY MORNING - ESTABLISHING SHOT

A State Highway Patrol car is parked at an intersection. The driver, DAVE, is watching traffic going along the highway. The second officer, BERT, is flipping through the day's briefing reports. Butcher in Olds approaches, goes past on highway. Dave looks after him, reacts.

> DAVE
> Bert - check the hot list for
> the license on that white job...

Bert checks quickly.

> BERT
> 4N85140...

Dave lets the car into gear rapidly - efficiently.

> BERT (cont'd)
> That it?

> DAVE
> Yep. Going south...

WIPE TO:

87 thru 89 SERIES OF SHOTS TO COVER CHASE

Patrol car run throughs, siren opening up. SOUND. Butcher spotting Patrol car, stepping on it. Butcher reaches side road turn-off, swings onto it - going fast.

WIPE TO:

90 thru 92 CHASE SHOTS - DIRT ROAD

Patrol car, gradually overtaking Olds. SOUND of siren wide open.

CUT TO:

93 EXT. COUNTRY ROAD - ESTABLISHING SHOT - COUPE

A teen-ager, driving his souped-up car at a good clip, radio blaring - unable to hear police siren - he's lost in his world of jive.

94 and 95 CUTS TO COVER

both Olds and coupe approaching curve - Patrol car after Olds, starts firing at tire.

96   ANGLE ON TIRE

   as it blows.

97   ANGLE ON OLDS

   Olds skids, comes to a stop, blocking road.

98   MED. SHOT

   as teen-ager swerves to avoid crash, comes to stop.
   Butcher gets out, sees nearness of police car, starts
   lumbering away. Patrol car brakes screech (SOUND) as
   it comes to a stop.

99   MED. CLOSE SHOT - TEEN-AGER (STILL IN CAR)

   He's unhurt but startled. He reacts to police, then -
   having good sense, he leaps from the car and takes to
   his heels.

100 MED. CLOSE SHOT - POLICE CAR

   The officers are spilling out of the car, guns in hand.
   One fires a shot into the air, shouts:

                    BERT
             Stop!

101 WIDE ANGLE

   Butcher continues running. The cops start after him - this
   time shooting at him, but low - hoping to get him in the
   legs.

102 CLOSE SHOT - BUTCHER

   He reaches an obstacle that trips him - a bullet hits the
   dirt beside him - another catches him in the leg - he
   staggers, stops - another bullet hits him in the shoulder.
   A look of astonishment spreads across his face - he puts a
   hand to his shoulder, to his leg - looks at the hand ---
   there is no blood. Slowly he turns around - another bullet
   smacks his chest - he looks down, bewildered, half-
   frightened - brushes his hand over spot - there is no
   damage. Examines holes in jacket.

103 CLOSE TWO SHOT - OFFICERS

   stopped in their tracks momentarily - amazed - unable to
   believe their eyes.

37.

104   CLOSE SHOT - BUTCHER

as he starts back toward them - a look of fiendish triumph on his face.

105   WIDE ANGLE

The Butcher moving towards them, slowly, inexorably.

>   BERT (WST)
>   (to Butcher)
>   Hold it.

The Butcher continues advancing.

>   DAVE (WST)
>   One of us must have hit him..!

>   BERT (WST)
>   We both have....

Both officers fire again - Butcher comes on.

106   LONG SHOT - TEEN-AGER

quite a distance away now, but he has stopped to look back - gapes at what he sees.

107   MED. SHOT - INCLUDING OFFICERS, BUTCHER

The officers stand their ground, taking aim and firing at Butcher as he closes in on them - the bullets taking no effect.

CAMERA MOVES IN to:

108   CLOSE SHOT - FAVORING BERT, BUTCHER

Butcher is nearest to Bert - only a few feet separating them.

109 * INSERT - BERT'S HAND, REVOLVER

Bert is emptying the gun point-blank at Butcher.

110   MED. CLOSE SHOT - ON BERT

reacting horrified. Butcher moving into shot - reaching for Bert - his back fills the screen. SOUND: screams.

                                              CUT TO:

38.

111   MED. ON TEEN-AGER

stopping to look back.

112   MED. CLOSE SHOT - PATROL CAR

its doors standing open - the police radio droning (SOUND).

      POLICE ANNOUNCER
   Car 63, come in please -- Car
   63....

Butcher comes into shot. The SOUND of the police radio
over:

      POLICE ANNOUNCER
   Car 63 - report in, please.

113   CLOSE SHOT - BUTCHER

as he examines himself where he was shot - puzzled, not understanding - then as the realization of his invulnerability hits him, he laughs hoarsely - triumphantly - throwing back his head.

      NARRATION
   Dr. Bradshaw's experiment was
   more effective than he could
   have dreamed -- The Butcher
   seemed indestructible - his
   tissue structure a solid mass
   of cells - like an alloy
   plating of metal but made of
   living, elastic flesh....

114   MED. SHOT

as Butcher goes to the teen-ager's coupe. He gets in the
coupe, starts it.

115   EXT. HIGHWAY - ESTABLISHING SHOT - COUPE RUN THROUGH

                FADE OUT:

FADE IN:

116   INT. POLICE STATION CORRIDOR - DAY - MED. SHOT - CHASEN

engrossed in newspaper, walks through. Several people
engrossed in work.

                (CONTINUED)

116   CONTINUED:

> NARRATION
> Back in Los Angeles, the
> headlines were beginning to
> scream when I reported in to
> the Police Station.

CUT TO:

117   INT. LAUDER'S OFFICE - MED. CLOSE SHOT - CHASEN

as Chasen opens door, goes in.

118   MED. SHOT

Lauder stands studying a map - which includes both San Francisco and Los Angeles. He looks around briefly, sees Chasen enter.

> LAUDER
> (short, but not
> unpleasant)
> You - and the rest of the force
> - are going on twenty-four hour
> duty....You've seen the
> headlines?

Chasen tosses paper on desk.

> CHASEN
> (responding like
> a fire horse)
> You mean this guy that's run
> amok up north?

Lauder nods, indicates the map - there are pins marking two spots.

> LAUDER
> Last report - he killed two cops
> - got away in a green coupe....
> Heading south. I've got a hunch
> he's going to be our baby. He
> could be in town right now.

Chasen nods.

> LAUDER (cont'd)
> Start things rolling.

Chasen starts to leave, Lauder sits down at desk, picks up reports. Chasen is at door when Lauder speaks again:

(CONTINUED)

118   CONTINUED:

                    LAUDER (cont'd)
               No leads on that holdup money?

                    CHASEN
                    (shakes head)
               I think the girl can probably
               be counted out. If any of
               the others are wise they're
               keeping it mighty quiet.

                    LAUDER
               Well, let it ride for now....
               The whole force is going to be
               on a spot till that killer is
               caught.
                    (grimly)
               The newspapers'll have a field
               day...

                                             CUT TO:

119   EXT. STAGE DOOR ALLEYWAY - PAN SHOT

        as the Butcher turns into the alleyway, past the shoeshine
        stand. Shoeshine boy is busy with a pair of shoes.

                                             WIPE TO:

120   INT. DRESSING ROOM - MED. SHOT

        Eva getting out of street clothes, automatically doing
        strip tease routine, humming the music.

121   INT. HALLWAY TO DRESSING ROOMS - MED. LONG SHOT

        SHOOTING FROM JUST OUTSIDE EVA'S DRESSING ROOM DOOR TOWARD
        OUTSIDE ENTRANCE where Butcher has just come in. Butcher
        comes TOWARD CAMERA. A stage hand and FRANCINE cross
        Butcher's path, but he comes steadily, ponderously TOWARD
        CAMERA.

                                             CUT TO:

122   INT. EVA'S DRESSING ROOM - MED. SHOT

        Eva is in her costume now and is hanging up her street
        clothes, standing by the wardrobe rack, her back to the
        door. The door swings open and Butcher comes through.
        Eva turns, her eyes go wide and her mouth opens, her face
        momentarily rigid with shock.

                                         (CONTINUED)

122   CONTINUED: (1)

> EVA
> Charles...

Butcher moves toward her - smiling. This is the one person he cares anything about - but the smile on the brutal face is anything but reassuring. Eva's mind begins to register again.

> EVA (cont'd)
> (slowly)
> It can't be! He's dead! But you look like him - only -- different, some way....

Butcher stands a few feet from her.

> BUTCHER
> It's me.

> EVA
> (frightened)
> I don't understand---

> BUTCHER
> (trying to explain)
> There was - a doctor - in San Francisco...
> (pauses, trying to think)
> I - don't know - but...

Eva moves to him, puts her hand on his arm as if to make sure she's not seeing things. She looks up into his face.

> EVA
> It is you.
> (simply)
> I'm glad you're - all right....
> But it's hard to understand...
> Why didn't the police tell me?

The Butcher laughs nastily - Eva reacts, alert, alarmed.

> EVA (cont'd)
> (softly)
> The police know, don't they?

> BUTCHER
> (laughs again)
> Maybe -- the -- dead ones -- should....

Butcher is amused by this.

(CONTINUED)

122 CONTINUED: (2)

> EVA
> (sharply, afraid)
> Charles! What have you done?
> (slowly)
> You've - killed someone since---?
> (her voice
> trails off)

Butcher lifts his hands, clenches them, proud.

> BUTCHER
> I'm strong, Eva -- <u>very</u> strong...

He wants to make her understand his great strength. His eyes spot a chair at Eva's make-up table. It has a back and legs of metal tubing. Butcher picks it up, twists it like it was putty.

> BUTCHER (cont'd)
> See?
> (boastfully)
> See, Eva?

Eva is fascinated and horrified. She nods.

> BUTCHER (cont'd)
> Even - bullets -- <u>can't stop
> me</u>...! The police - don't
> matter --- It's going to be
> real nice, Eva.

The Butcher drops the chair. Eva takes a step back from Butcher, her face mirroring her horror. Butcher's interest shifts.

> BUTCHER (cont'd)
> But I got things to do. Have
> you done anything about getting
> the money?

> EVA
> (near tears)
> What money?

> BUTCHER
> The six hundred thousand!

Eva shakes her head. Butcher studies her a moment, intently, then he reaches out, grabs her arm.

> EVA
> (shakes head,
> puzzled)
> I don't know anything about it.

(CONTINUED)

122   CONTINUED: (3)

                    BUTCHER
                (scowling, sus-
                  picious)
            You - trying - to rat on me
            too?

Eva reacts instantly to his words, her free hand lashes
out, slaps him sharply. Butcher drops her arm, surprised.
His hand goes to his cheek.

                    EVA
            Don't you talk to me like that!

Butcher stares a moment - then, angered, he pushes her....
not hard, but it's enough to send her crashing against the
wall. Eva whimpers in pain and fear, but she's got real
nerve.

                    EVA (cont'd)
                (glares through
                  her tears)
            You are mean. Everyone always
            said so - I didn't believe it...

Butcher stares, then shakes his head as though trying to
remember something - confused.

                    BUTCHER
                (more to himself)
            I - don't want to hurt you...
                (frowns, then re-
                  membering money)
            Didn't you read the message I
            left?

Eva is still frightened.

                    EVA
                (keeping control,
                  puzzled)
            There wasn't any message - just
            a fifty dollar bill....

                    BUTCHER
                (ominously)
            No!

                    EVA
                (protesting)
            It was, Charles. I opened the
            envelope last night - after Paul
            left....

Butcher adds the piece, slowly:

                                            (CONTINUED)

122 CONTINUED: (4)

          BUTCHER
Paul - knew....? About the
message...?

          EVA
Not till last night. I hadn't
told anyone. You said not to...

123 CLOSE SHOT - BUTCHER

          BUTCHER
         (figuring it, angry)
Paul...!

124 MED. CLOSE TWO SHOT

His expression softens as he looks at Eva.

          BUTCHER
Sure. You wouldn't rat on me.
You're the only one I can
trust...

Butcher moves to Eva who stands her ground in spite of her
fear. Clumsily he strokes her shoulder, then turns to
leave.

          EVA
         (barely whispering)
What are you going to do?

          BUTCHER
         (pausing, to
          answer)
Get Squeamy - Joe - Paul....
I said I would....

          EVA
         (pleading)
Charles - don't....

          BUTCHER
I'll be back...Then - just you
and me - anything you want----

Butcher goes on to door, opens it, looks back.

          BUTCHER (cont'd)
I'll be back....

Eva shudders as the door closes after Butcher - she stands,
staring. O.s. SOUND of his heavy footsteps retreating.
Eva leans back against dressing table - weak.

                                        WIPE TO:

45.

125   EXT. STAGE DOOR ALLEYWAY - MED. SHOT

    as Butcher comes out, turns north and walks, unhurriedly.
    SOUND of heavy footsteps.

                                                                   CUT TO:

126   INT. HALLWAY OUTSIDE EVA'S DRESSING ROOM DOOR - MED. SHOT

    There is a wall phone just outside her door. She comes
    out, clutching a robe over her scanty costume, hesitates
    a moment looking at phone and then hurries on.

                                                                   WIPE TO:

127   EXT. STAGE DOOR ALLEYWAY - SHOESHINE STAND - MED. SHOT

    Eva comes running from b.g. into f.g. of shot to shoeshine
    stand, looks around on the street quickly, speaking to the
    shoeshine boy.

128   MED. CLOSE TWO SHOT - EVA, SHOESHINE BOY

    Shoeshine boy looks at her - eyes popping. O.s. SOUND of
    wolf whistle. Eva looks down at costume, realizes how she
    is dressed - runs back down alley.

129   EXT. STREET - MED. SHOT - BUTCHER

    continuing down street.

                                                                     CUT TO:

130   INT. HALLWAY - MED. CLOSE SHOT - EVA

    (SOUND of Butcher's heavy footsteps carrying over as music
    b.g.) As Eva reaches the wall phone outside her dressing
    room door. She has a coin, inserts it in coin slot, and
    dials. Francine, a buxom, dark-haired dish, dressed in a
    filmy costume, comes up to Eva.

                          FRANCINE
                     (chewing gum)
        Eva - can I borrow your eyebrow
        pencil?

    Eva brushes her away, then gets the question, nods and in-
    dicates dressing room. Francine goes into the dressing
    room.

                                                                     CUT TO:

46.

131   EXT. STREET - BUTCHER WALK THROUGH

                                            LAP DISSOLVE TO:

132   INT. HALLWAY - DAY - MED. CLOSE SHOT - EVA

hanging up - inserting coin - dialing. Phone rings at other end.

                        EVA
                    (urgently)
            Joe!

                                            CUT TO:

133   INT. SQUEAMY-JOE ROOM - MED. CLOSE SHOT - SQUEAMY

reacting - fearfully.

                        SQUEAMY
                    (interrupting)
            Joe's not here - this is
            Squeamy.
                    (listens)
            What'd you say about Benton?

He listens again to Eva's frantic voice a moment, sweat breaking out on his forehead.

                        SQUEAMY (cont'd)
                    (interrupting
                     again)
            You mean he hired a killer---?
            Benton's dead...

Eva is trying to explain, but Squeamy goes right on talking - over the SOUND of her voice.

                        SQUEAMY (cont'd)
            That guy can't even let his own
            bones rest easy....
                    (voice rising with
                     a note of hysteria)
            Hiring a killer to get us! I'll
            try to warn Joe and Paul---

Squeamy hangs up, cutting off the SOUND of Eva's voice. He mops his face, gulping, sees bottle of liquor on table --- drinks a big swig from it.

                                            CUT TO:

134   INT. HALLWAY - MED. CLOSE SHOT - EVA

looking at the telephone receiver, realizing Squeamy has hung up - that he didn't understand her. She breaks the connection, gets another dime from handbag and dials the operator. She's near tears.

                    EVA
            Get me the police!

She waits, trying to control her sobs. Francine sticks her head out the dressing room door, starts to ask something - Eva doesn't see her - Francine stares curiously, realizing Eva's in quite a state, then shrugs her shoulders, disappears back into dressing room.

                    EVA (cont'd)
                (into phone)
            Lt. Chasen, please - hurry!
                (listens)
            Oh - when will he be back?
                (listens)
            Yes----
                (thinks a moment)
            Tell him Charles Benton is alive
            and bullets won't stop him!
            He'll know what to do...!
                (listens, shouts
                  back into re-
                  ceiver)
            I'm not crazy! What?
                (pause, thinks)
            Just say I'm----
                (biting lip)
            ---a friend of Charles....
                (starts hanging
                  up receiver)
            He'll know....

Eva leans her head against the instrument a moment.

                                        CUT TO:

135   INT. DRESSING ROOM - MED. SHOT

* Francine is helping herself to all of Eva's make-up. Eva comes back through the door, pushes it shut and leans against it, her eyes closed, completely unaware of Francine. Francine furtively pushes the make-up jars back in place, turns around, looks at Eva curiously, crosses to her.

                    FRANCINE
                (hopefully)
            You sick?

                                        (CONTINUED)

135 CONTINUED: (1)

Eva starts, opens her eyes.

>> EVA
> What?

Francine reacts, disappointed. Eva crosses to dressing table, leans her weight on her two hands placed on table.

>> FRANCINE
>> (still hopeful)
> You don't look so good to me.

From o.s. nasal voice calls out:

>> VOICE (o.s.)
> Ten minutes, Eva.

>> EVA
>> (automatically)
> All right.

>> FRANCINE
> Say - Eva - I could take over the matinee trick for you.

Eva looks at her, not really listening.

>> EVA
>> (vaguely)
> What?

>> FRANCINE
>> (urgently)
> Eva - I can do it - Look!

She does a few quick struts and bumps. Eva looks at her as if just becoming conscious of her.

>> EVA
>> (with decision)
> Francine...! I just thought of something.

>> FRANCINE
> Yeah?

>> EVA
> You'll have to take over the matinee for me.

Francine reacts in hurt surprise. Eva starts getting out of costume, clumsy with haste.

(CONTINUED)

135   CONTINUED: (2)

                    FRANCINE
          What do you think I been
          beatin' my gums about....
                  (realizing,
                   joyous)
          I can? Gee - thanks - I'll
          go tell Hank.

   Francine opens the door and exits, slamming it after her.

                                                  CUT TO:

136   EXT. STREET - MED. SHOT - BUTCHER

   walking. SOUND of footsteps over.

                                                  CUT TO:

137   INT. LAUDER'S OFFICE - MED. SHOT

   SOUND of Butcher's heavy footsteps carrying over and fading. Lauder and the Desk Sergeant are comparing fingerprints. Chasen comes in.

                    CHASEN
          You want me, Captain?

                    LAUDER
          We just got a rundown on the
          fingerprints in the stolen
          car. Nothing on the driver,
          who was killed, or the woman
          with him. But take a look
          at these.

138   INSERT - FINGERPRINTS

139   MED. SHOT

   Chasen leans over to look. Lauder points to the prints on
   the right.

                    LAUDER
                  (continuing)
          These are the killer's...

                    CHASEN
          They look the same to me---

   Lauder reaches behind him.

                                              (CONTINUED)

139   CONTINUED: (1)

>   LAUDER
>   The file prints are Butcher
>   Benton's.
>
>   CHASEN
>   (startled)
>   What? How do the lab boys
>   explain that?
>
>   LAUDER
>   (shrugs)
>   They don't - their best guess
>   is a twin brother - an identical
>   twin could have the same pattern
>   of whorls with only slight
>   variations. Ever hear of the
>   Butcher having a brother?
>
>   CHASEN
>   No.

Lauder and Chasen stare at each other, each thinking.

>   SERGEANT
>   (suddenly, re-
>   membering)
>   Benton! That reminds me. I
>   forgot to tell you, Lieutenant
>   ---some whacky dame phoned for
>   you. Left a message. Said to
>   tell you...
>   (quoting)
>   "....Charles Benton is alive
>   and----
>   (exaggerated
>   sarcasm)
>   --bullets won't stop him!"

Chasen and Lauder react.

>   LAUDER
>   If we buy the twin theory....
>
>   CHASEN
>   (to Sergeant)
>   Who was she? Where'd she see
>   him?
>
>   SERGEANT
>   Wouldn't give her name - sounded
>   hysterical to me. Said she was
>   a friend of the Butcher's.

Chasen looks at Lauder.

(CONTINUED)

51.

139   CONTINUED: (2)

                    CHASEN
                (wondering)
            Eva Martin?

He starts for the door.

                    SERGEANT
                (ruefully)
            Some guys have all the luck
            - I never drew a detail at
            the Follies.

Chasen shrugs and grins, goes out the door.

                                        DISSOLVE TO:

140   EXT. STAGE DOOR ALLEYWAY - DAY - SHOESHINE STAND - MED. SHOT

      as Chasen enters shot heading into alleyway. Shoeshine boy
      looks up from paper he's reading.

                    BOY
            Shine, Lieutenant?

Chasen doesn't stop as he answers:

                    CHASEN
            Not now - I'm busy....

                    BOY
                (calling after him)
            Business or pleasure?

                                        WIPE TO:

141   INT. EVA'S DRESSING ROOM - DAY - MED. SHOT

      Eva moves about the dressing room restlessly. She is fully
      dressed now. SOUND of a light knock on door. Eva freezes.

                    EVA
                (weakly)
            Who is it?

                    CHASEN (o.s.)
            Dick Chasen....

Eva rushes to door, flings it open, throws herself into
Chasen's arms with a sob of relief. Chasen is surprised
by the violence of her greeting but very pleasantly so.

                    EVA
            Dick! He's coming back----

                                        (CONTINUED)

141 CONTINUED: (1)

Chasen edges Eva inside the room, his arm around her, pushes door shut behind him.

>   CHASEN
>   Steady now. Who's coming back?

Eva pulls away a little to look at him.

>   EVA
>   (wildly)
>   Charles Benton. Didn't you
>   get my message?

>   CHASEN
>   (interrupting,
>   gently)
>   Now, honey. The Butcher is
>   dead. Did he have a brother
>   --- a twin brother?

>   EVA
>   Oh, no! Charles was here --
>   don't you think I'd know him?

Chasen pulls her close to him.

>   CHASEN
>   (soothingly)
>   There, honey. You've had a
>   bad time.

She looks up at him, frantic, wanting to make him believe.

>   EVA
>   (hurrying on,
>   tightly)
>   He's going to kill Squeamy -
>   and Joe - and Paul....He'll
>   get the money----and....

>   CHASEN
>   (interrupting
>   quickly)
>   He knows where the money is?

>   EVA
>   (impatiently)
>   Of course!

>   CHASEN (cont'd)
>   (forcefully)
>   That $600,000 damn near cost me
>   my job - I'm going to get it and
>   maybe another killer as well.

(CONTINUED)

141   CONTINUED: (2)

>   CHASEN
>   (thinking rapidly;
>   I'll get a tail on those guys--
>
>   EVA
>   (interrupting,
>   yelling)
>   Don't you understand? It
>   isn't another killer - it's
>   Charles Benton!
>
>   CHASEN
>   (firmly)
>   Baby, Benton was executed at
>   five o'clock yesterday afternoon
>   --- get that through your head.
>   (more gently,
>   concerned)
>   I better take you over to the
>   Station - get someone to look
>   after you....

Eva bites her lip in vexation.

>   EVA
>   (very definite)
>   No!
>
>   CHASEN
>   (worried about
>   her, dubious)
>   Well---I'll get a man staked
>   out here, too -- as soon as
>   I can -- in case this killer
>   comes back....

Eva nods her head dully. Chasen starts to door, turns back.

>   CHASEN (cont'd)
>   (trying again)
>   You're sure?

Eva nods. Chasen takes her by the shoulders.

>   CHASEN (cont'd)
>   I hate to leave you alone.

He kisses her quickly, lightly - turns and exits.

142   CLOSE SHOT - EVA

looking after him - startled.

DISSOLVE TO:

143   INT. SQUEAMY-JOE ROOM - DAY - MED. SHOT

Squeamy has his gun on the table, the bottle is nearly empty. He paces the room nervously, picks up the gun, moves to look out the window over which he has the shade drawn. He empties the bottle, throws it in the wastebasket. Suddenly he freezes at the o.s. SOUND of footsteps coming down the hall outside his door. Squeamy looks frantically around, makes his decision. He pockets gun, goes to the window, pulls up the shade and slides through window onto the fire escape.

CUT TO:

144   INT. HALLWAY - ESTABLISHING SHOT

ESTABLISHING the footsteps are those of another man going to his room.

CUT TO:

145   EXT. FIRE ESCAPE - SQUEAMY - ESTABLISHING SHOT

ESTABLISHING him reaching pathway from fire escape - he goes down path, the SOUND of his light footsteps picking up from the SOUND of footsteps in cut above.

CUT TO:

146   EXT. BOTTOM OF ANGEL'S FLIGHT - MED. SHOT - BUTCHER

He gets on cable car.

CUT TO:

147   EXT. ANGEL'S FLIGHT - MED. LONG SHOT - SHOOTING DOWN

ESTABLISHING the two cars passing.

WIPE TO:

148 *   INT. SQUEAMY-JOE ROOM - MED. SHOT

as the Butcher comes in. SOUND: footsteps. He looks around, turns and goes out unhurriedly.

CUT TO:

149   INT. EVA'S DRESSING ROOM - MED. SHOT

Eva moves about the room restlessly.

(CONTINUED)

149 CONTINUED:

Francine comes in - clad in flashy, abbreviated costume.

>   FRANCINE
>   (probing)
>   Gee - you're not dressed.
>   You going some place?
>
>   EVA
>   (absently)
>   What? -- Oh ... I don't know.
>   (to herself)
>   I don't know _what_ to do....
>
>   FRANCINE
>   (hopefully)
>   Want me to take the next stint
>   too?
>
>   EVA
>   (impatiently)
>   I - don't - care!

Francine is amazed and shocked. This is blasphemy.

>   FRANCINE
>   What!

Suddenly Eva makes up her mind.

>   EVA
>   (firmly)
>   Francine, I _am_ going out.
>
>   FRANCINE
>   (pleased)
>   Does that mean I do the next
>   show?

Eva nods - and exits hurriedly.

                                             CUT TO (?)

150 EXT. BRADBURY BUILDING - DAY - ESTABLISHING SHOT - SQUEAMY

Squeamy hurries along, stops at entrance to building as if debating going in - changes mind and goes on to bar and enters.

                                             WIPE TO:

151 INT. BAR - DAY - MED. SHOT

There are only two or three customers in the place.

                                             (CONTINUED)

151   CONTINUED:

The woman lush, seen earlier, is drinking alone at far end of bar. Squeamy comes in, sidles quickly up to the bar. As Bartender comes over to him, he speaks softly, anxiously:

> SQUEAMY
> Seen Joe Marcelli?
>
> BARTENDER
> (coldly)
> Not since last night when I told him not to come around here again.
>
> SQUEAMY
> Gimme a shot.

Bartender pours shot, shoves it over toward Squeamy, who downs it, signals for another. Squeamy keeps looking over his shoulder toward the door, nervous - jumpy. Bartender gives him the second shot.

> SQUEAMY (cont'd)
> Seen Paul Lowe?

Bartender shakes his head as we....

CUT TO:

152   EXT. STREET - MED. SHOT - BUTCHER

TO ESTABLISH him walking toward Bradbury Building and Bar. SOUND of footsteps - the effect we want is a momentary tension over whether he is going on past Bradbury Building to Bar. He pauses at entrance to Bradbury Building, then goes in.

CUT TO:

153   INT. BAR - MED. SHOT

Squeamy is leaning across the bar toward Bartender.

> SQUEAMY
> (low, but very
> nervous)
> I - need help - just found out Benton hired a killer to get me. He's after Joe too - and....

(CONTINUED)

153   CONTINUED:

                        BARTENDER
                     (tensing, hard,
                      cutting in)
                Then drink up and get out. I
                don't want trouble in my place.

                        SQUEAMY
                     (sarcastically)
                You're a real pal----

                        BARTENDER
                     (quickly)
                Drink up and get out, I said---

        Squeamy drinks up, slams jigger on the bar, starts out.
        Bartender moves down bar to woman lush, nodding his head
        in direction of Squeamy to indicate he's discussing him
        with woman.

                                                    WIPE TO:

154   EXT. BRADBURY BUILDING ENTRANCE - MED. SHOT

        as Squeamy enters. SOUND of his light, scuttling foot-
        steps.

                                                    CUT TO:

155   INT. FIFTH FLOOR GALLERY CORRIDOR - MED. SHOT - BUTCHER

        walking up to Paul's office. SOUND: heavy footsteps.

                                                    CUT TO:

156   INT. BRADBURY LOBBY - ELEVATOR - MED. SHOT

        as Squeamy gets into elevator, starts it up.

                                                    WIPE TO:

157   INT. FIFTH FLOOR GALLERY CORRIDOR - MED. CLOSE SHOT -
        BUTCHER

        coming out of Paul's office - leaving door ajar - moving
        toward elevator.

158   ANOTHER ANGLE

        TO ESTABLISH elevator with Squeamy in it, is almost at
        fifth floor.

159   MED. CLOSE SHOT - SQUEAMY

as he opens door, starts out of elevator, sees Butcher, backs into elevator, slams door shut, tries to start elevator down.

160   REVERSE TOWARD BUTCHER (THROUGH GRILL)

as he wrenches open grill door.

>   BUTCHER
>   Rat on me, would you, Squeamy?

161   MED. CLOSE TWO SHOT

Squeamy has gun out, starts shooting at Butcher as Butcher comes into cage after him.

                                               CUT TO:

162   MED. SHOT - TOWARD OFFICE DOOR - MAN WITNESS

as Man Witness comes out, stops, horrified at what he sees. SOUND of gunfire over.

                                               CUT TO:

163   MED. SHOT - TOWARD ELEVATOR

as Butcher hauls Squeamy out of elevator cage.

                                               CUT TO:

164   LONG SHOT - DOWN TOWARD LOBBY - WOMAN ATTENDANT

looking up - alarmed - reacts.

                                               CUT TO:

165   MED. SHOT - TOWARD RAILING

as Butcher lifts Squeamy above head.

166   LONG SHOT - BODY

hurtling down - SOUND of Woman Attendant's screams over.

167 MED. SHOT - TOWARD BUTCHER

as he begins to walk toward stairway - unconcerned.

                                                CUT TO:

168 MED. CLOSE SHOT - WOMAN ATTENDANT AT PHONE

                    WOMAN ATTENDANT
                (yelling into
                  phone)
            Police...!

169 MED. SHOT - STAIRWAY - BUTCHER

as he reaches stairway, unhurriedly starts down.

                                             DISSOLVE TO:

170 INT. BRADBURY BUILDING LOBBY - DAY - MED. SHOT

The Woman Lush has forced her way toward an Officer, is trying to demand his attention - finally she makes the grade.

                    WOMAN LUSH
            It was Charles Benton, I tell
            you...He went right by me---
                (illustrates)
            ---close as this!

                    MAN WITNESS
            I can tell you all about it.
            Look, I see this big----

                                                CUT TO:

171 MED. SHOT

TO ESTABLISH Butcher's heading toward Angel's Flight again.

                                                CUT TO:

172 INT. BRADBURY BUILDING ENTRANCE - MED. SHOT

The entrance to the building is clogged by the curious - being held back by a policeman. Eva comes up street - reacts in surprise and alarm as she sees the group by the entrance. She hurries up to the group.

                                             (CONTINUED)

172 CONTINUED:

> NARRATION
> Eva hurried to Paul's office,
> planning to wait there, hoping
> to get a chance to warn him---

173 MED. CLOSE SHOT - EVA, TWO OR THREE BYSTANDERS, BARTENDER

as Eva tries to see over them to see what's happened. She reacts as she hears one bystander speak to another.

> EVA
> What's happened?

> BARTENDER
> Guy named Squeamy - got thrown
> from the fifth floor ---
> deader'n a mackerel.
> (wonderingly)
> Customer of mine!

> EVA
> (sharply)
> Do you mean Squeamy Ellis?

The Bartender twists his neck to look back at her.

> BARTENDER
> Yeah - that's it....

> EVA
> (apprehensively)
> He didn't kill anybody else?

> BARTENDER
> (big take)
> Isn't one enough?!

Eva turns away - the Bartender looking after her shaking his head.

DISSOLVE TO:

174 * INT. LOBBY - MED. GROUP SHOT - DAY - LAUDER, CHASEN, MAN WITNESS

> MAN WITNESS
> I tell you - the bullets never
> even fazed him.

> COP
> Must be wearing a bulletproof
> vest.

(CONTINUED)

174 CONTINUED:

> LAUDER
> (bitterly,
> to Chasen)
> God help us when <u>this</u> hits the
> papers.
> (to cops)
> Keep a man here.

Lauder turns back to Chasen.

> LAUDER (cont'd)
> We'll get a stake-out on Joe
> Marcelli....

> CHASEN
> I'd like to talk to Joe.
> (thinking)
> Maybe I better phone San Quentin.
> Suppose Benton could be alive---

DISSOLVE TO:

175 EXT. TOP OF ANGEL'S FLIGHT - DAY - TOWARD CABLE CAR - ESTABLISHING SHOT

as Eva gets out of cable car, walks along railing, watching both upper and lower levels. She is very nervous.

> NARRATION
> Eva felt it was up to her to
> warn Paul and Joe. Here on
> Bunker Hill was the room
> Squeamy shared with Joe. Eva
> hoped she'd be in time to save
> him....

176 MED. SHOT - **SQUEAMY**-JOE ROOM - P.O.V.

ESTABLISHING Butcher appearing at door leading out to fire escape landing. He steps out on landing.

177 MED. CLOSE SHOT - EVA

reacting to seeing him. She moves quickly back behind palm, out of sight of Butcher....With effort, she forces herself to remain, keep lookout for Joe.

178 CUTS TO ESTABLISH PROWL CARS (T. CARS) - TOURING AREA
and
179 Prowl car driving in, stopping north end of Olive.

CUT TO:

62.

180   EXT. BRADBURY BUILDING - CHASEN AND LAUDER

They come out of building, walk to prowl car.

CUT TO:

181   EXT. TOP OF ANGEL'S FLIGHT - MED. SHOT

Eva - getting more scared and anxious by the moment - suddenly spots Joe just starting across intersection on Hill Street below. She starts to yell, glances toward window and thinks better of it. She runs to get on cable car - gets through turnstile and into car, waits impatiently for it to start, trying to keep sight of Joe.

As the cable car goes down with Eva on it, ESTABLISH that Joe has crossed to alleyway north of flight and started up it. Eva spots him, realizes he will reach the top and the entrance to the apartments before she can reach him. Butcher is not at the window right at this moment. Eva tries frantically to get Joe's attention, but he neither sees, nor hears her, but plods steadily on up the alleyway.

182   MED. SHOT - BUTCHER

coming out on fire escape platform. He sees:

183   MED. LONG SHOT - BUTCHER'S P.O.V. - JOE

Joe on pathway under fire escape.

184   CLOSE SHOT - BUTCHER

He smiles, steps back inside.

185   MED. SHOT - TOP OF ANGEL'S FLIGHT - EVA, PASSENGERS

Eva is delayed in getting out by the other passengers.

186   * MED. SHOT - ENTRANCE OF ROOMING HOUSE - BUTCHER

He's waiting for Joe who has reached top of pathway. Butcher cannot be seen by Joe. Joe walks to steps of porch before Butcher steps into his view. Joe reacts, turns - heads for stairway NORTH of rooming house. Butcher follows.

187 CUTS TO COVER STAIRWAY
thru
189
Joe going down stairway. Butcher in to shot and after him. Joe stumbles - goes down - Butcher reaches him - Joe tries ineffectually to fight Butcher off with crutch.
Eva gets to foot of stairway - on Clay Street - in time to witness Butcher hurling Joe down stairway.

190 MED. SHOT - PROWL CAR - OLIVE STREET

one officer running toward stairway. The other is talking into radiophone - excitedly.

> OFFICER (WST)
> ---he's our man...!

191 MED. SHOT - SHOOTING DOWN STAIRWAY

Butcher, convinced Joe is dead, starts up stairway - meeting officer running down - slams officer out of way, breaking his arm. SOUND: approaching sirens.

192 MED. SHOT - CLAY STREET - EVA

running SOUTH away from bottom of stairway toward stairway under cable cars. Chasen and Lauder -- in prowl car -- are heading toward her. Another prowl car - the one just seen on Olive Street - is coming down Clay Street from the north.

193 CLOSE SHOT - CHASEN, LAUDER

Chasen has recognized Eva.

> CHASEN
> (to driver)
> Pull over - it's Eva!

194 MED. SHOT

TO ESTABLISH the car swerving over, pulling to a stop. Chasen is out and running for Eva before it stops rolling. Eva is turning into pathway beside and underneath Angel's Flight - Chasen catches her a few steps below Clay Street.

195 MED. CLOSE SHOT - EVA, CHASEN

as Chasen grabs her. Before she sees who it is she gasps out:

(CONTINUED)

195   CONTINUED:

> EVA
> (panicky)
> Let me go - let me go..!

> CHASEN
> Eva - stop it!

Eva recognizes him, goes limp against him.

> EVA
> (hysterically)
> He's - killed - Joe, too!
> Stay away from him, Dick.

196   MED. SHOT

Chasen half-carries, half-walks Eva back to the F. car, puts her in between Lauder and himself.

CUT TO:

197   FULL SHOT

ESTABLISHING T. CAR (prowl - black and white) coming down Clay southbound, to pull to a stop at foot of no. stairway where Joe has been killed. The officer leaps out, heads up stairs. F. car pulls up alongside T. car - Chasen and Lauder leap out.

CUT TO:

198   LONG SHOT - SHOOTING DOWN NO. STAIRWAY

Officer Driver kneels beside injured officer. Chasen and Lauder race up to them, past Joe's body.

199   MED. CLOSE SHOT

The injured officer's pain is secondary to his mental distress.

> INJURED OFFICER
> (bitterly)
> He killed a man right in front
> of my eyes, and I couldn't stop
> him!

Officer Driver turns to race on up stairway.

65.

200   MED. SHOT - OFFICER DRIVER

as he comes back down.

                    CHASEN
                  (calling)
            Did he get away?

                    OFFICER
            Yeah --- in a pick-up truck!

                                                    CUT TO:

201   EXT. FREEWAY - LONG SHOT

ESTABLISHING the freeway in a traffic jam.

202   CLOSE SHOT - PAUL LOWE

sitting at the wheel of his car, blocked in traffic jam. He switches on car radio, lights a cigarette as SOUND from radio up.

                    ANNOUNCER
            ---and the police have not
            issued an official statement
            but a reliable source informs
            me that one man - a superhuman
            fiend - is believed responsible
            for this trail of destruction
            from San Francisco to Los
            Angeles. A blood-chilling
            sequel to this afternoon's
            murder of Squeamy Ellis....

Paul reacts violently.

                    ANNOUNCER (cont'd)
            ...is the statement of a witness
            that the killer...
                  (voice underlines)
            Get this - the witness claims
            the killer is Charles - the
            Butcher - Benton - a man who
            was legally executed in San
            Quentin yesterday afternoon!

Paul's face mirrors his incredulity, fright. As the newscast continues, Paul gets in a real sweat to get going -- looks anxiously ahead to see what's holding up traffic, adds the noise of his horn to the angry blasts of protesting motorists around him.

                                                    CUT TO:

66.

203 EXT. STREET - RUN THROUGH

   ESTABLISH Butcher driving pickup truck.

   DISSOLVE TO:

204 INT. EVA'S DRESSING ROOM - NIGHT - MED. SHOT - PAUL

   Only the dressing table lights are on - the rest of the room is dark. Paul sits in chair against wall on hinged side of door. Door is open, screening him, he smokes nervously. O.s. SOUND of finale music. Francine enters, switches on lights, then sees Paul, gasps:

>   FRANCINE
>   (startled)
>   Oooooooh!
>   (recognizing him)
>   You gave me a start, Mr. Lowe.
>
>   PAUL
>   (sternly)
>   What're you doing in here?
>   Where's Eva...?
>
>   FRANCINE
>   (misunderstanding,
>   on the defensive
>   -- pouty)
>   I'm taking her place so I'm
>   using her costumes. What's
>   it to you?
>
>   PAUL
>   (sharply)
>   I asked you - where's Eva?
>
>   FRANCINE
>   (assuming her ver-
>   sion of a Marilyn
>   Monroe stance,
>   mouth open)
>   Watch your tone of voice, Buster
>   ...I told you, Eva isn't here.
>
>   PAUL
>   (annoyed)
>   I can see that for myself! Where
>   is she?
>
>   FRANCINE
>   (waving her hand
>   airily, indif-
>   ferently)
>   At Police Headquarters - that's
>   where she is....

(CONTINUED)

204   CONTINUED:

>   PAUL
>   (reacting,
>   surprised)
>   Why?
>
>   FRANCINE
>   (tossing her head,
>   shrugging)
>   I don't know. She phoned, said
>   where she was and that I should
>   go on for her tonight----
>   (vivacious now)
>   You going to catch tonight's
>   show?

Paul has already started toward door.

>   PAUL
>   (sarcastically)
>   Some other time - when there's
>   something I want to see...!

Paul exits - it takes a couple of beats before his answer registers. She snorts indignantly as we...

                                        DISSOLVE TO:

205   INT. LAUDER'S OFFICE - NIGHT - MED. SHOT

Eva sits at the desk - a cup of coffee in front of her. Chasen stands beside desk chair, talking on phone, his attitude indicating the person on the other end is a VIP.

>   CHASEN
>   ----yes, sir ----- No, sir,
>   Captain Lauder is still with
>   the Mayor....The killer's
>   dropped out of sight - he was
>   last seen in the Hollywood
>   area.
>   (listens)
>   Yes, sir, we know he's dangerous
>   - every angle is being covered,
>   sir.
>   (listens)
>   Yes, sir, I'll tell him.

He hangs up phone, looks at Eva.

>   CHASEN (cont'd)
>   (heartfelt)
>   Whew!

                                        (CONTINUED)

205 CONTINUED: (1)

He walks to window - looks out. Desk Sergeant opens door, puts his head in. SOUND of much activity from outside - teletype bells, jumble of voices, footsteps, etc.

> DESK SERGEANT
> Any idea how soon the Captain'll be back?

Chasen shakes his head. Paul moves into position so that he can be seen over Desk Sergeant's head.

> PAUL
> (loud, determined)
> I'm going to see the Captain if I have to wait all night!

Eva reacts, coming to her feet.

> EVA
> Paul!

Paul, hearing her voice, pushes on through past the Desk Sergeant. The Desk Sergeant steps inside doorway.

> EVA (cont'd)
> (urgently,
> to Paul)
> Paul! Charles killed Squeamy and Joe!

> PAUL
> (shaken)
> Joe, too!
> (suddenly reacting)
> Charles....Benton?!

> EVA
> (near tears)
> He's alive - I saw him - but nobody will believe me....

> CHASEN
> (deliberately)
> I'm checking it. My guess is - whoever killed them - is on the trail of the money, Lowe. Maybe you'd better start talking if you know anything about it.

> PAUL
> (still dazed)
> I - don't know anything---

(CONTINUED)

205   CONTINUED: (2)

>   CHASEN
>   (pushing it)
>   Did the Butcher have a brother?
>
>   PAUL
>   No - no brother....
>
>   EVA
>   (hoping to con-
>   vince Paul)
>   Paul - it's <u>Charles</u>!
>
>   PAUL
>   (gulping, think-
>   ing fast)
>   I - demand - police protection!
>
>   CHASEN
>   (prodding)
>   Where's the money, Lowe?

Paul holds himself together with effort.

>   PAUL
>   You heard me - I demand police
>   protection. I know my rights.
>
>   CHASEN
>   (coldly)
>   We've put stakeouts on your
>   office and apartments.
>
>   PAUL
>   (firmly)
>   That's not enough.
>
>   CHASEN
>   (equally firm)
>   That's enough as far as we're
>   concerned.

Paul lights a cigarette, stalling for time, thinking ---
Suddenly he turns to Desk Sergeant standing behind him.
Deliberately, he smashes his fist in Sergeant's face,
catching him unawares. Eva gasps. Sergeant rolls back
from blow, comes back like an angry bull, grabs Paul
roughly.

>   PAUL
>   (quickly - shaken,
>   but pleased)
>   You going to book me, Sergeant?

(CONTINUED)

205   CONTINUED: (3)

                    SERGEANT
                  (furious)
          And throw away the key!

Paul throws Chasen a victorious grin as Sergeant escorts
him roughly out of room.

                                              CUT TO:

206   EXT. SUMP AREA - NIGHT - MED. SHOT

      ESTABLISHING Butcher and pickup truck behind some shrubbery
      - which would conceal truck from road.

                    NARRATION
              Butcher had headed for a sump
              pit north of San Fernando
              Valley - where a year before
              he had ditched the armored car
              and the six hundred thousand
              dollars - under twenty feet of
              water. Now that Paul knew the
              whereabouts of the money,
              Butcher expected him to come
              after it. He hid his car and
              waited. The hours ticked off,
              Paul didn't appear....

                                              WIPE TO:

207   SAME SHOT

      Butcher starts truck, turns on lights - drives to edge of
      sump pit.

                    NARRATION
              The Butcher got restless --
              decided to get the money....

      Butcher gets out of car, gets chain from back of pickup
      truck.

                    NARRATION (cont'd)
              The Butcher had a personal
              interest in this holdup loot
              - Or maybe he just didn't
              realize that money was no
              longer a problem for him,
              that he could take what he
              wanted when he chose ----

                                              DISSOLVE TO:

71.

208 EXT. HILLSIDE NEAR SUMP PIT - NIGHT - ESTABLISHING SHOT - A DIRT TURNOUT

A light-colored car is parked, the lights switch off.

209 INT. CAR - MED. CLOSE SHOT - BOY, GIRL

The girl snuggles close to the boy.

          GIRL
       (smiling up at him)
  Our favorite spot....

Boy takes her in his arms - their kiss is long and enthusiastic. He releases her slightly.

          BOY
       (murmuring in
        her ear)
  Been a long time---

          GIRL
       (giggling,
        pleased)
  Since last night....

Boy suddenly pushes her a little farther away, looks directly at her.

          BOY
       (pleadingly)
  Ginny - we can't go on like
  this....

She turns her head, frowning.

          GIRL
       (evasively)
  It - won't be for much longer...

Boy releases her, sinks back against the seat, sighs. He is facing o.s., toward sump area in this position. He sits brooding a few moments until his attention is caught by something he sees o.s. below. He leans forward, looking, curious.

          BOY
  Look - someone's down there....

The girl looks too.

                            CUT TO:

72.

210 LONG SHOT - TOWARD SUMP PIT - P.O.V.

Butcher's car headlights are shining on the water - the silhouetted figure of Butcher on ledge above water - he is hauling away on chain - darkness blots out any other details.

211 INSERT - CHAIN

coming out of water.

                     CUT TO:

212 INT. COUPE - MED. CLOSE TWO SHOT

      BOY
     (puzzled)
Looks like something being
hauled out of the sump --
something heavy. I can't see
a derrick though - funny there
aren't more lights....

The Girl has lost interest - is once more engrossed in her own problems.

      GIRL
Uh-huh.
     (persuasively)
Honey, if I tell him now, <u>he'll</u>
be the one to get the divorce.
If we wait---

      BOY
     (interested only
      in girl friend
      now)
Wait! Wait! I'm tired of
waiting. What diff----

      GIRL
     (cutting in,
      voice edgy)
You said you'd be patient...

      BOY
     (raising voice)
I have been!

      GIRL
     (also raising
      voice)
It's as difficult for me----

                     CUT TO:

213 INT. LAUDER'S OFFICE - NIGHT - MED. SHOT

Eva is looking out window, dejectedly; Lauder is at phone as Chasen enters, reports in his hands. SOUNDS: from outer office as door opens - activity.

> LAUDER
> (into phone)
> All right - all right..!

He slams the phone down - looks at Chasen who has crossed to the desk.

> LAUDER (cont'd)
> Anything new?

> CHASEN
> (ticking it off)
> Report on Dr. Bradshaw - the owner of the station wagon. The San Francisco Police located his laboratory in the basement of an electrical power receiving station---

> LAUDER
> (impatiently)
> Bradshaw - what's he know?

> CHASEN
> He's dead - and another man too -- his assistant. The lab is a shambles....

Eva interrupts.

> EVA
> (distressed)
> Charles mentioned a doctor....

Chasen glances at her and then looks back at Lauder.

> CHASEN
> (voice carefully under control)
> There's still another report from San Francisco. Benton's body never arrived at the mortuary where it was supposed to go. An attendant there finally broke down, admitted he picked up some quick cash by handing the body over to a man he was unable to identify ...<u>The man was driving a station wagon</u>....

(CONTINUED)

213 CONTINUED:

Lauder's nerves are on edge. He breaks in now, explosively:

                    LAUDER
      Damn it all, man - the Chief's
      on my neck - the Comissioners're
      on <u>his</u> and the Mayor's on <u>theirs</u>.
      Am <u>I</u> supposed to tell them the
      killer is a dead man!

Before Chasen can reply, the Desk Sergeant bursts into room.

                    SERGEANT
      Captain. Report from the Valley
      on a hysterical woman.....
      reports the presence of the
      killer----

Lauder, Chasen, Eva react. Lauder starts for door, Chasen after him.

                    LAUDER
               (to Chasen)
      Come on.

                    EVA
            (frightened for them)
      Please - be careful!

Lauder and Chasen reach door, open it.

                                         WIPE TO:

214 EXT. POLICE GARAGE - NIGHT - LAUDER'S CAR - RUN THROUGH

ESTABLISHING Lauder and Chasen out.

Other police cars exiting garage.

                                       CUT TO:

215 EXT. SUMP AREA - NIGHT - MED. CLOSE SHOT - PICKUP TRUCK, BUTCHER

Butcher is throwing a sack of money into the truck where a pile of other sacks are already stacked. The sacks are wet. Butcher gets in truck, starts it.

                                       WIPE TO:

216 EXT. DIRT ROAD - RUN THROUGH

                                       WIPE TO:

217   EXT. CAVE - NIGHT - ESTABLISHING SHOT - TWO ENTRANCES

as the Butcher drives in beside cave, stops, gets out. He takes several sacks of money - goes into cave, reappears to get some more.

> NARRATION
> Butcher chose the abandoned
> quarry nearby as a temporary
> hiding place for the money
> so he could continue his
> search for Paul Lowe.

218   INT. CAVE - ESTABLISHING SHOT

DISSOLVE TO:

219   EXT. ROAD NEAR ELECTRICAL STATION - NIGHT - RUN THROUGH

TO ESTABLISH Chasen and Lauder passing Electrical Station or close enough to it so towers are visible. SOUND: sirens.

CUT TO:

220   EXT. CAVE - MED. SHOT - BUTCHER

coming out of cave for more sacks. He takes the last of them from the truck.

DISSOLVE TO:

221   EXT. SUMP AREA - NIGHT - MED. SHOT

Several police cars are on the spot. The road has been blocked off.

222   EXT. SQUAD CAR - MED. CLOSE SHOT

The girl - Ginny - is seated in car, hunched over, rocking back and forth - her eyes and hair wild. Convulsive sobs rack her from time to time. Lauder and Chasen are with her.

> LAUDER
> (gently, prod-
> ding her)
> --- so you and your boy friend
> had a fight and he got out to
> take a walk....

(CONTINUED)

222   CONTINUED:

Girl nods.

> LAUDER (cont'd)
> You noticed that he started walking in the direction of the sump where you'd both seen lights a short time before....

Girl nods.

> LAUDER (cont'd)
> All right. What happened then? Please try to tell us.

Girl nods again, trying to pull herself together.

> GIRL
> (speaks with difficulty)
> I - just sat there - a few minutes I guess - I was pretty mad. Then there was a loud crash - like heavy metal, sort of - from down here. I got out of the car to get a better look.
> (buries face in hands a moment)
> I heard Billy cry out something -- I couldn't make out the words but down here - in a patch of light - was Billy. And - coming toward him - was - this man. A big man - he lifted Billy up above his head like he didn't weigh a thing - Billy screamed - just once - before he broke Billy's back....
> (shudders, nearly losing control again)
> I heard it - snap - that far away --- Then I started running until I found a house -- they let me use a phone....

She stops, the sobs racking her again. Lauder rises, looks at Chasen.

> LAUDER
> (to Girl)
> Thanks, Miss. We'll send you home now.

He gestures to Chasen and they move out of shot.

CUT TO:

223   MED. SHOT - ARMORED CAR

The metal still gleams wetly - the car is flooded with light from police car spots. The doors of the car yaw open, twisted and bent. Several officers make way for Lauder and Chasen.

> LAUDER
> (to one of the men)
> Got a report on the fingerprints?

> OFFICER
> They match.

Lauder nods, indicates doors to Chasen.

> LAUDER
> Bent them like they were cardboard....

Chasen is examining the doors too. He looks at Lauder.

> CHASEN
> And how do you explain this?
> (motioning to armored car)
> He didn't have any heavy equipment - there aren't any tracks....

> LAUDER
> (slowly)
> That's right....

> CHASEN
> Maybe we better go along with her version - and deal with this killer as if he does possess superhuman qualities.

Lauder has been reluctant to make this decision. Now that he must make it, he does so decisively - once again he is an able, efficient machine.

> LAUDER
> (firmly)
> All right. We'll call in the special squad - heavy equipment...
> (thinking fast)
> Keep our stakeouts on - Send out a city-wide alert that no one is to try to take this man until we're ready----

(CONTINUED)

223   CONTINUED:

> CHASEN
> What about the general public?
> I suppose they'll have to be
> warned....

The two men stare at each other - knowing what this will mean.

> LAUDER
> (sighing)
> I suppose so. There's a would-be
> hero in every crowd.

Chasen starts for nearest police car as we....

DISSOLVE TO:

224   EXT. POLICE STATION CITY HALL - NIGHT - MED. SHOT

ESTABLISHING Lauder and Chasen arriving in police car, entering building.

CUT TO:

225   EXT. STREETS - CUTS TO COVER

Butcher driving pickup through deserted streets.

> NARRATION
> The City was alerted -- all
> citizens warned to stay off
> the streets unless on urgent
> business. The Butcher had
> been spotted, but...

226   EXT. STREET CORNER - RUN THROUGH

ESTABLISHING Butcher going past street corner - a police car is parked at the intersection - makes no move to follow him.

> NARRATION
> ....he went his way unmolested
> ....but the reports kept us
> informed of his direction....

WIPE TO:

227   EXT. ANOTHER STREET CORNER - RUN THROUGH PICKUP TRUCK

79.

228   CLOSE SHOT - BUTCHER

   driving. O.s. SOUND from radio.

                    RADIO ANNOUNCER
              Let me remind you again - stay
              off the streets. The police
              have taken Eve Martin - Follies
              dancer friend of the Butcher -
              and his former lawyer, Paul
              Lowe, into protective custody...

   Butcher looks sullen, angry. He wheels steering wheel over
   savagely.

                                              DISSOLVE TO:

229   INT. HALLWAY TO CELL BLOCK - NIGHT - ESTABLISHING SHOT

   Chasen and Eva going away FROM CAMERA along hallway to cell
   block at rear.

230   MED. CLOSE SHOT

   as Eva and Chasen stop at cell. Paul is in cell - he comes
   to barred door.

                    CHASEN
              We're mobilizing all available
              men and equipment to trap the
              Butcher. If you know anything
              that might help, now's the time
              to spill it.

   Paul shrugs.

                                              CUT TO:

231   INT. POLICE GARAGE TOWARD MAYOR'S ELEVATOR - ESTABLISHING
       SHOT

   as Butcher arrives at elevator - police elevator operator
   frowns, starts to question the Butcher, suddenly recognizes him.

                                              WIPE TO:

232   INT. HALLWAY OF JAIL FLOOR - TOWARD ELEVATOR

   as elevator doors open - Butcher steps out. The body of
   the policeman lies crumpled on elevator floor.

                                              CUT TO:

233 INT. CELL BLOCK - LONG SHOT

past desk, etc., in f.g., toward barred cells in b.g. Eva and Chasen are talking through bars to Paul. Three policemen are in room, variously occupied. All alert to o.s. SOUND of gunshots, start hurrying to door, police drawing guns.

234 ANOTHER ANGLE

as Butcher bursts through door. Policeman nearest door opens fire. Butcher knocks him aside. Second policeman exchanges revolver for tear gas gun -- gets in a short burst before he, too, is knocked aside. Then the third officer as he rushes in to attack....Chasen stops short, holding his ground, gun drawn, which is Eva's chance to catch up with him, hurl herself in front of him.

      EVA
 No - no!

Chasen pushes Eva aside, leaps for the Butcher but is knocked aside and he, too, crumples to the floor - unconscious....Butcher goes on past Eva who has backed against a cell door.

235 MED. SHOT - FAVORING PAUL

as Butcher approaches his cell. Paul is backed against far wall of cell, babbling his terror:

      PAUL
 Benton - I'm your friend - I
 didn't double-cross you....

Butcher shoves outstretched hands against bars - they give way - Butcher's huge frame - his hands still outstretched - blots out view of Paul as he continues toward him.

236 MED. CLOSE SHOT - EVA, CHASEN

Eva is leaning over Chasen, anxiously trying to bring him to. She freezes at o.s. SOUND.

      PAUL (o.s.)
    (wailing)
 No-o-o....

His voice rises to a shriek, breaks off.

237 MED. SHOT - EVA IN F.G., CELLS IN B.G.

Eva, still crouched over Chasen, looks toward Paul's cell.

(CONTINUED)

237   CONTINUED:

Butcher comes out of it, moves toward Eva. Eva rises as Butcher reaches her, starts backing away. She is crying softly, hopelessly.

>   BUTCHER
>   We - can - go - now - Eva...

Eva shakes her head - Butcher seems surprised, but he picks her up easily, continues toward door. Eva struggles, fighting, as he carries her down the corridor screaming hysterically.

                                        DISSOLVE TO:

238   INT. POLICE CAR - NIGHT - MED. CLOSE SHOT - LAUDER, CHASEN

Lauder is driving. Chasen's head is bandaged - They are listening intently to reports coming in over radio.

>   VOICE ON RADIO
>   ...Barham Blvd. on to Olive,
>   heading north ----
>
>   CHASEN
>   (thoughtfully)
>   He might be heading back into
>   the Valley foothills -- But
>   why....

Lauder shakes his head.

>   ANOTHER VOICE ON RADIO
>   Car 91 reporting. Pickup truck
>   just passed Riverside Drive
>   intersection, continuing north
>   along Olive----

Chasen suddenly gets idea, speaks into radio phone:

>   CHASEN
>   (into phone)
>   Car 91 - calling Car 91....
>
>   VOICE ON RADIO
>   Car 91 here, sir---
>
>   CHASEN
>   (into phone)
>   Does he have any kind of gear
>   stored in that truck - suitcases,
>   cloth bags.....? Over---

                                        (CONTINUED)

238   CONTINUED: (1)

                  VOICE ON RADIO
        Car 91 here, sir. No gear in
        bed of truck, sir....

                  CHASEN
             (to Lauder,
              pointedly)
        He stashed that money some
        place after he got it out of
        the armored truck----

                  LAUDER
             (voice edgy
              with eagerness)
        Out in that same area - that
        what you're thinking?

                  CHASEN
        It's a possibility...

                  LAUDER
        Give me that phone.

Lauder takes phone, driving with one hand.

                  LAUDER (cont'd)
             (into phone)
        Get me the Fire Chief....

                  VOICE ON RADIO (CHIEF KARGER)
        Karger speaking.

                  LAUDER
             (into phone)
        Lauder here.....If we can corner
        our man out near the sump pit
        area, will you buy it?

                  KARGER
             (over radio)
        Trap him in that area and we can
        give you full cooperation. You
        can throw the works at him there.

                  LAUDER
        Start your men out - Squad cars
        will check, lead them in....

Lauder hands phone back to Chasen.

                  LAUDER (cont'd)
             (to Chasen)
        Start it rolling.

(CONTINUED)

238   CONTINUED: (2)

>   CHASEN
>   (tight, remind-
>   ing him)
>   You've got to let me get Eva
>   out before you open up on him.
>
>   LAUDER
>   (pointedly)
>   If you can---
>
>   CHASEN
>   (grimly)
>   I will...

Chasen raises phone to mouth, to start issuing orders.

(NOTE: Shots of fire trucks, police cars, etc.?)

                                              DISSOLVE TO:

239   EXT. CAVE - NIGHT - MED. SHOT

TO ESTABLISH pickup truck parked near south entrance of the cave. Butcher putting sacks of money in truck. He goes back into cave. Truck lights shining into cave.

                                              CUT TO:

240   EXT. ROAD ABOVE CAVE AREA - ESTABLISHING SHOT - POLICE CAR

TO ESTABLISH car has come to a halt - officers looking o.s. down to:

241   LONG P.O.V. - CAVE AREA

The pickup truck can be plainly seen.

                                              WIPE TO:

242   CUTS TO COVER
thru
244   TO ESTABLISH police and firemen surrounding area - quietly - afoot - carrying flame throwers, tear gas guns, bazookas.

245   CUTS TO COVER
thru
247   cars parked out of sight of cave entrances.

84.

248　CLOSE SHOT - CHASEN

　　　ESTABLISH him with tear gas gun.

249　CLOSE SHOT - LAUDER, FIRE CHIEF

　　　ESTABLISH them - watching.

250　MED. LONG SHOT - CHASEN P.O.V.

　　　Chasen edging up around truck to cave entrance.

251　CUTS TO COVER
thru
254　men with flame throwers, etc., moving silently in closer.

255　CLOSE SHOT - CHASEN

　　　beside truck - alert - listening. From o.s. inside cave -
　　　SOUND of Eva beginning to sob softly. Chasen freezes....
　　　waiting - listening.

　　　　　　　　　　　　　　　　　　　　　　　　CUT TO:

256　INT. CAVE - MED. CLOSE SHOT - BUTCHER, EVA

　　　Eva sighs deeply, begins to recover from hysteria, opens
　　　her eyes slowly, sees Butcher - cringes away, terrified.
　　　Butcher is surprised by her attitude - wants to reassure
　　　her.

　　　　　　　　　　　　BUTCHER
　　　　　　　　　　(with difficulty)
　　　　　　　Everything - is - all right -
　　　　　　　now ----- Eva.

　　　He starts to pat her hand, Eva shrinks farther away.

　　　　　　　　　　　　BUTCHER (cont'd)
　　　　　　　　　　(puzzled)
　　　　　　　Don't be - afraid...It's - _me_...

　　　Eva stares at him, eyes wide.

　　　　　　　　　　　　BUTCHER (cont'd)
　　　　　　　What's wrong?

　　　He takes her hand, she jerks it away.

　　　　　　　　　　　　EVA
　　　　　　　　　　(with loathing)
　　　　　　　Don't - touch me...

　　　　　　　　　　　　　　　　　　　　　　　(CONTINUED)

256   CONTINUED:

                        BUTCHER
                        (harshly)
                Eva!

    Eva makes a sudden move to duck under his outstretched arm.
    Instinctively he grabs for her. She struggles as he lifts
    her, his immense strength hurting her, though he doesn't
    intend to. Eva crumples against him, whimpering with pain.
    Butcher reacts, frightened - sets her on her feet, holding
    her away from him, peering at her.

                        BUTCHER (cont'd)
                        (anxiously)
                I - don't *want* to hurt you....

    Eva is near the breaking point - exhausted, becoming re-
    signed to anything that might happen. She lifts her head,
    stares at Butcher coldly.

                        EVA
                        (slowly, de-
                        liberately)
                I - never believed anyone could
                be so - horrible...

                        BUTCHER
                        (wildly, hurt)
                No! Eva - no - don't say that!

    Then - wanting to convince Eva and himself, he takes her by
    the shoulders, shakes her - gently.

                        BUTCHER (cont'd)
                You're all that matters...!

                                                    CUT TO:

257   EXT. CAVE - SOUTH ENTRANCE - NIGHT - TRUCK, CHASEN

    TO ESTABLISH Chasen edging into cave past truck. He keeps
    close to wall of cave and out of beam of headlights until
    he is a few feet past front of truck and into cave.

                                                    CUT TO:

258   INT. CAVE - MED. SHOT OVER CHASEN - TOWARD BUTCHER, EVA

    Chasen steps deliberately into shaft of light, tear gas gun
    held ready.

                        CHASEN
                        (sharply)
                Benton!

86.

259   ANOTHER ANGLE

Butcher turns slowly away from Eva. Eva cries out:

> EVA
> Dick - get back - he'll kill you!

Chasen stands perfectly still, silhouetted in the beam of the headlights as Butcher moves toward him. Chasen waits until Butcher is within a few feet of him, then shoots tear gas directly into Butcher's face. Butcher reels back, blinded and infuriated. Chasen ducks past him, grabs Eva by the hand, half-drags her out through the north entrance of cave.

                                                    CUT TO:

260   EXT. NORTH ENTRANCE - MED. SHOT

TO ESTABLISH police with flame throwers, bazookas, moving into cave as Eva and Chasen come out.

261   EXT. SOUTH ENTRANCE - MED. SHOT

TO ESTABLISH police and equipment moving in here also - past truck.

262   INT. CAVE - SHOTS TO COVER
thru
264   Flame throwers, bazookas opening up on Butcher.

ESTABLISH Butcher rolling to put out flames.

ESTABLISH Butcher charging out through north entrance of cave in spite of stuff being thrown at him.

                                                    CUT TO:

265   EXT. CAVE - MED. SHOT - CHASEN, EVA, LAUDER, FIRE CHIEF

standing some distance away from north entrance of cave as Butcher comes out. ESTABLISH their horror - incredulity at seeing him. Butcher is still somewhat blinded, then sees them, starts for them. Chasen, thinking fast, grabs Eva's hand, starts running around bend, shouting to Lauder:

> CHASEN
> Let him follow us----

87.

266   ANOTHER ANGLE

TO ESTABLISH Butcher plunging after Chasen and Eva, roaring with rage as Lauder shouts to men:

>   LAUDER
> Don't try to stop him----

Chasen and Eva reach car parked below bend. Chasen pushes her into Patrol Car.

267   CLOSE SHOT - BUTCHER

TO ESTABLISH him, realizing he can't catch them as the engine turns over. He turns back.

268   LONG SHOT

TO ESTABLISH Butcher going back for truck - the police fall back - let him alone as Lauder's shouts direct them to. Butcher backs the truck - turns and heads out.

269   ANOTHER ANGLE

TO ESTABLISH Chasen has deliberately stalled so Butcher can follow. Now, seeing Butcher in truck coming - he guns ahead.

270   INT. PATROL CAR

>   CHASEN
> I need your help, Eva---

Eva nods.

271   CUTS TO COVER
thru
274   Butcher chasing patrol car.
Lauder and Fire Chief following in Chief's car.
Chasen driving with siren wide open.
Butcher driving like a maniac.

275   SERIES OF CUTS TO ESTABLISH
thru
277   Chasen and Eva heading for Power Station.
Butcher following.
Patrol cars, etc., following, but keeping back.

278   MED. CLOSE TWO SHOT - EVA, CHASEN IN CAR

Eva is looking back over shoulder.

(CONTINUED)

278 CONTINUED:

Chasen speaks into radio phone.

>   CHASEN
> Lauder....it's a long shot
> but here's what I'm going to
> try----

                                        WIPE TO:

279 MED. LONG SHOT

as Chasen wheels the patrol car into the dead end street at the Power Station. He and Eva pile out of the car, run for the gate. Butcher's car roars into shot. He slews car around as he sees it's a dead end, comes to a skidding stop. Butcher gets out of car, starts after Eva and Chasen. Then, seeing where they are heading, Butcher hesitates.

280 MED. CLOSE TWO SHOT - EVA, CHASEN

Chasen looks back, sees Butcher has hesitated outside gate.

281 LONG SHOT - INCLUDING CHASEN, EVA, BUTCHER

>   CHASEN
>   (shouting, taunting)
> You'll never get her, Butcher!

Butcher comes charging after them.

282 SERIES OF CUTS TO ESTABLISH:
thru
285 The Chase, on foot, through the Station grounds.

Shots to establish Chasen trying to figure how to maneuver.

INTERCUT arrival of Lauder, police, firemen, etc. They stay outside the Station grounds.

286 LONG SHOT

ESTABLISHING Chasen heading for Gantry Crane, leading Eva. Butcher after them.

287 CUTS TO COVER
thru
290 Chasen and Eva along catwalk to far end. They wait until

(CONTINUED)

287 CONTINUED:
thru
290 Butcher reaches catwalk, then Chasen nods to Eva. She runs down stairway at far end. Chasen along ramp leading to control house. Chasen starts Gantry Crane moving the moment Eva jumps clear.

The Crane gathers speed. Chasen out, jumps for grappling hook, swings to ground moments before Crane slams against barrier. There is a tremendous flash - the Crane tilts, crashes.

FADE OUT:

FADE IN:

291 INT. LAUDER'S OFFICE - DAY - MED. SHOT - CHASEN, LAUDER

Chasen is speaking into dictaphone, finishing report.

                CHASEN
    ...and the tremendous shock of
    electricity that brought the
    Butcher back to life destroyed
    him. That was my big gamble -
    it payed off.

Chasen pauses, passes a hand over his eyes, wearily.

              CHASEN (cont'd)
    The $600,000 stolen in the
    Armored Truck robbery has
    been recovered. Case closed.

Chasen puts the dictaphone instrument back on hook, looks at Lauder as he indicates notebook.

              CHASEN (cont'd)
    Here's the scientists' notebook
    for your records....I had to
    fill in a few spots with my own
    conjecture - but that's about
    the size of it.

Lauder nods.

              LAUDER
      (sympathetically)
    Get any sleep since the business
    last night?

Chasen gets up, stretches.

              CHASEN
    Some - not much.

(CONTINUED)

291   CONTINUED:

Chasen moves to the window, looks out as he lights a cigarette.

               LAUDER
     How's the Martin girl today?

               CHASEN
     Called the hospital about an
     hour ago....She'd gone---

               LAUDER
       (surprised)
     Gone? Where?

Chasen turns to look at Lauder, smiling wryly.

               CHASEN
       (shrugs)
     She told them she was a working
     girl - and she'd been away from
     the job too long already.

               LAUDER
       (approving;
        pointedly)
     Quite a girl, eh, Chasen!

               CHASEN
     Yeah.
       (sighs)
     Say, how about that time off
     I've got coming?

               LAUDER
       (grins)
     Two weeks - starting right now -
     get some rest - see some sights.

               CHASEN
       (grinning back)
     Maybe I will....

                             DISSOLVE TO:

292   EXT. BURLESQUE HOUSE - NIGHT - MED. SHOT

Chasen is standing in front of the cardboard cutout of Eva, much as he was in opening shot.

293   MED. CLOSE SHOT - CHASEN

He is studying the cutout thoughtfully. With the thoughtful expression still on his face, he turns away toward the box office.

294 MED. CLOSE SHOT - AT BOX OFFICE

as Chasen walks up to the box office, shoves some money in, gets a ticket. He turns INTO CAMERA, looking at the ticket, still thoughtful, then as he starts to move toward the entrance, a slight smile starts as we....

                                         FADE OUT:

T H E   E N D

The Music of *Indestructible Man*
By David Schecter

At first glance, analyzing Albert Glasser's music for *Indestructible Man* would seem to be a fairly easy job, given that the composer's writing was usually straightforward and not very musically complex. However, the seeming simplicity of the task was a fleeting impression. A search through the inventory of Glasser's music archive in Wyoming failed to turn up any recordings of music for the picture, and he was usually very thorough at saving recorded copies of his scores in one condition or another. Perhaps more surprising was that no music manuscripts pertaining to *Indestructible Man* could be found either, as he took great pride in saving his written scores for posterity. As the film was one of his first monster movies, and starred Lon Chaney (who also appeared in an earlier Glasser-scored picture, 1951's *The Bushwhackers*), one might have expected he would have saved documents pertaining to *Indestructible Man*, as Glasser likely would have considered this a prestigious B-picture assignment worthy of preservation.

That *Indestructible Man* was not an important project for Glasser becomes apparent when consulting his 434-page self-published autobiography *I Did It!!* Although he wrote more about certain scores and pictures in his book than others, he not only failed to write anything about *Indestructible Man*, he didn't even mention it in any of his memoir's lists of what films he worked on during various phases of his life.

If you aren't familiar with Glasser's compositional style, you'd never know it's his music in *Indestructible Man* because he didn't receive a screen credit, unlike

Albert Glasser must have scored a hit with Jack Pollexfen, Bert I. Gordon and other low-budget producers, as he worked regularly on their movies—amidst dozens of others—in his 20-year Hollywood career.

earlier Pollexfen-produced films he scored like *Port Sinister*, *The Neanderthal Man* and *Captain John Smith and Pocahontas*. It just so happens that nobody received any screen credit in *Indestructible Man* pertaining to the music, not even for a "Music Supervisor" or "Musical Director." When films don't credit a composer, they often credit one of those two positions, which refer to the person who conducted the score at the recording session, or else the executive who runs the music department for a studio or the music business affairs for an independent picture.

A film would also sport one of those two credits when a score was written by multiple composers, as it wasn't considered a virtue when too many writers were involved in one score. However, it's more likely that music executives just gave this as an excuse so they could get their own names up on the screen instead of the actual people who wrote the music. The same credits can also be found when scores were assembled from compositions written for prior movies, a process called "tracking." And this credit could occur whether the earlier compositions were freshly recorded by an orchestra or if the actual old recordings were re-used. This re-use of previous recordings usually—but not always—occurred in low-budgeted pictures produced by small production companies. In these cases the music supervisor or one of his underlings would select various cues from their library of recordings and then a music editor would assemble them in the soundtrack and fade them in and out to try to fashion a dramatic score that wouldn't sound too out-of-place in its new uses. It took a lot of effort to get such a musical assemblage right, because there would almost always be mismatches between the recordings and the new scenes the music was supposed to accompany. While generic romantic melodies were usually suitable for the new romantic scenes, and one chase could easily substitute for another, when there was something out of the ordinary in a library cue, such as a sudden orchestral eruption that matched some visual in its original incarnation, that same eruption could call attention to itself in its new use when there was no corresponding image for it.

Glasser worked on so many cheap pictures that he sometimes worked with his own duplicated music, having extra copies of the same recordings made to be used in multiple places in a film. This saved time and money because you could get two or more music cues by recording only one piece. Sometimes he would also re-use recordings from his earlier films, combining them with original music to fashion a "new" soundtrack. Because of this, when watching a Glasser film it's not always easy surmising where some of the music might have come from. This isn't made any easier because the composer's music could sound very similar from picture to picture, as he had a definite style and a similar approach to scoring many of his pictures. And his orchestrations were seldom diverse enough where you could tell that different cues might have derived from different films.

While it's not definite that every last drop of music in *Indestructible Man* was written by Glasser, all of it certainly sounds like him in terms of composition, orchestration and even conducting. Although some of the music has been traced to earlier movies that Glasser worked on, most of it has not. It's sometimes easy to tell if older recordings originally written for earlier pictures have been re-used in a later film due to the different sound quality, visual-to-musical mismatches, and musical edit points. But if the music was wisely chosen and cleverly edited, sometimes it's more difficult than one might think. There are a few cues in *Indestructible Man* that fit the visuals like a noisy glove, and there's always the possibility that a handful of pieces were composed by Glasser especially for the film. But there's no evidence of that. The film's cue sheet list 27 separate pieces of music, all of them titled to match the *Indestructible Man* action. However, because cues known to have been written for earlier movies are given new titles related to the plot of *Indestructible Man*, the cue sheets offer no way of knowing if any compositions were actually written for the picture.

The fact that nobody received any music credit in the picture suggests that it might be an all-tracked score compiled from previous recordings, and those in charge might have been hiding that fact, since such a practice was frowned upon by the Musicians' Union. If all the music was old, that would certainly explain the absence of any physical artifacts associated with the picture such as recordings or music manuscripts.

In addition to fabricated cue names, the June 15, 1955, cue sheets show many incorrect timings, often a sign that they were hastily assembled without any regard for accuracy. There are pieces heard in the movie that have no matches on the cue sheets, and many cues heard in the movie start or end abruptly, or else fade in or out in an unnatural way. These are all clues that previous recordings were being used, although some messiness in a soundtrack can always be attributed to editing being done to the film after the music was added to the film. The cue sheets show 51:40 of music in *Indestructible Man*, whereas a French cue sheet lists the entire score as 6:12 in length. If the latter document

```
                                077  0653
   MUSIC CUE SHEET

      Production No. _____          Date  JUNE 15, 55

      Photoplay entitled   "THE INDESTRUCTABLE MAN"  (1955)

      Produced by    CORWIN-GROSS-KRASNE-PRODUCTIONS

      Studio         CALIFORNIA

      Producer    JACK POLLEXFIN       Musical director   ALBERT GLASSER
```

REEL 1.   TIMING

1. Composition MAIN TITLE   Partial _____ Entire 1:00
   Composer   ALBERT GLASSER   Inst. Bkgd. X Vocal Bkgd. ___
   Publisher   AMERICAN ACADEMY OF MUSIC INC. Inst. Visual __ Vocal Visual __

2. Composition AT THE PRISON   Partial _____ Entire :17
   Composer   ALBERT GLASSER   Inst. Bkgd. X Vocal Bkgd. ___
   Publisher   AMERICAN ACADEMY OF MUSIC INC. Inst. Visual __ Vocal Visual __

3. Composition "I'M GOING TO KILL YOU"   Partial _____ Entire :22
   Composer   ALBERT GLASSER   Inst. Bkgd. X Vocal Bkgd. ___
   Publisher   AMERICAN ACADEMY OF MUSIC, INC. Inst. Visual __ Vocal Visual __

4. Composition NEWSPAPER HEADLINE   Partial _____ Entire :20
   Composer   ALBERT GLASSER   Inst. Bkgd. X Vocal Bkgd. ___
   Publisher   AMERICAN ACADEMY OF MUSIC, INC. Inst. Visual __ Vocal Visual __

5. Composition THE BURLESQUE HOUSE   Partial _____ Entire 1:47
   Composer   ALBERT GLASSER   Inst. Bkgd. X Vocal Bkgd. ___
   Publisher   AMERICAN ACADEMY OF MUSIC, INC. Inst. Visual __ Vocal Visual __

6. Composition BACKSTAGE   Partial _____ Entire 2:05
   Composer   ALBERT GLASSER   Inst. Bkgd. X Vocal Bkgd. ___
   Publisher   AMERICAN ACADEMY OF MUSIC, INC. Inst. Visual __ Vocal Visual __

7. Composition THEY BRING IN THE BODY   Partial _____ Entire 2:50
   Composer   ALBERT GLASSER   Inst. Bkgd. X Vocal Bkg. ___
   Publisher   AMERICAN ACADEMY OF MUSIC, INC. Inst. Visual __ Vocal Visual __

8. Composition BENTON COMES BACK TO LIFE   Partial _____ Entire 3:40
   Composer   ALBERT GLASSER   Inst. Bkgd. X Vocal Bkgd. ___
   Publisher   AMERICAN ACADEMY OF MUSIC, INC. Inst. Visual __ Vocal Visual __

The *Mystery Science Theater* gang are about halfway into *Indestructible Man*'s opening credits when one of them says of the cacophonous excuse for music, "Sounds like the soundtrack is *drunk*!" Pictured: Page one of the movie's three-page cue sheet.

was used to calculate international royalties for Glasser through the years, it would have resulted in him being substantially underpaid for his music.

Assuming that the music in *Indestructible Man* was originally written for productions predating it, analyzing the music from a compositional standpoint pertaining to how it worked in the movie makes no sense, since it wasn't written to be heard in that context. Such an evaluation would be more of a critique of the job done choosing which particular library cues would be used in the picture and whether the music spotter, music editor and music mixer did a good job incorporating the old music into the movie. Inappropriate music doesn't sound quite so unsuitable when its volume is diminished, or when the more inappropriate parts are deleted from the surrounding material. But not knowing what musical material they had to choose from in the first place makes that approach shortsighted, too. Evaluating the music cues from a purely compositional standpoint unrelated to how they're used in the movie is also not going to be fair to the composer, since you'd have no idea what original images he was writing the music to fit. Plus, only a section of an original cue is likely to have been used in its new context. In other cases, what you think might be one composition could, in fact, be various passages from unrelated cues strung together to create the impression that the music is one cue written for a single dramatic situation.

It's hard enough evaluating Glasser's music even when you're certain he wrote a completely new score for a picture, as his dramatic instincts were not very subtle. Much of his music could sound over-the-top in terms of composition and orchestration, and while this worked better during action and science fiction-horror settings, sometimes his music could be just as unrestrained during less-dramatic situations when other composers would have reduced the intensity a lot or perhaps not used any music there in the first place. So even when Glasser composed music for a specific sequence, his music could stand out for the wrong reasons. This makes it even tougher guessing whether any audio-to-visual mismatches are the result of somebody sticking a totally inappropriate piece of music to a new scene, or whether Glasser himself didn't do a sterling job of dramatically accentuating the footage. And in those cases where the music perfectly matches the visuals, if we're being honest, music composed by any composer will often work very well in a completely different setting. That makes it more difficult than one might think when guessing whether a given piece is original or not.

Because of all these caveats, probably the best way of discussing the music in *Indestructible Man* is from the standpoint of how the music works in the picture, regardless of whether the score was actually written for the movie or whether it was assembled from a sea of unrelated cues from prior productions. Regardless of the size of the music library used to score *Indestructible Man*, and whether Glasser or somebody else chose them, there were probably certain reasons why the cues heard in the movie were selected above others. In the instances where there's at least some minimal possibility that cues might have been written and recorded specifically for *Indestructible Man*, it's probably okay to go out on a limb and analyze them from that perspective. If it is later discovered they weren't written for the picture, then it's a sign that whoever chose that music found some excellent library cues that matched the new contexts extremely well.

Music plays a large role in *Indestructible Man* if only because, for reasons we may never know, there are scenes where the characters' dialogue was discarded and replaced by Lt. Dick Chasen narration. The music probably helps add some dramatic underpinning to these particular spots. And because the movie has threadbare production values, the underscore manages to impart a bit of perceived value to the proceedings.

Indestructible Man opens with a typical Albert Glasser "Main Title," one which could fit a wide variety of genres, perhaps even an "Oriental movie." In fact, this particular cue served as the "Main Title" for the 1947 PRC series entry *Philo Vance Returns*, and the version used in *Indestructible Man* appears to be the same recording, only in edited form to match the shorter title sequence in the horror film. Instead of basing his opening statement on a long melody, much of the composition repeats a short, semi-melodic statement with some minor variations. The piece lacks any discernible structure, and instead is more or less an assemblage of various phrases, an approach Glasser's writing often took. The cue almost sounds like it could have been composed by Miklós Rózsa, after he'd had a few too many drinks.

As was often the case with Glasser's music, his ambitions could surpass both the orchestral forces at his disposal as well as his talent as a composer. Some of his orchestrations were rather clumsy, as he would occasionally have too much going on simultaneously for the number of instruments as his disposal. When working with a small ensemble of about 20 players, it's often best to keep things simple. The strings in the "Main

Title" are clearly being pushed to their limit, as Glasser needed a larger string section that would have provided a more mellifluous sound when trying to get that much volume out of them. This didn't appear to bother him, as he often seemed to mainly be going for *loud*!

The messiness of the piece could be due to its composition, orchestration, conducting or the performance by the orchestra, but it's more than likely due to one or more of the first three rather than the fourth, as even low-budgeted movies generally used extremely professional musicians who could get the job done fast and with minimal mistakes. The unrelenting composition tried to add some excitement to the very unexciting *Philo Vance Returns*, and it almost suits *Indestructible Man* even better due to it being more of an action picture.

One of the first musical clues that we're dealing with a tracked score is after the "Main Title" ends and a shot of the Hall of Justice appears. The short cue that's heard isn't listed on the cue sheets, and it was obviously not recorded at the same sessions as the previous piece, as it has a much different, brighter sound to it. As most older film scores were performed in one session at a single recording studio, all of the pieces should be sonically similar. These first two pieces clearly aren't.

The gentle cue "At the Prison" is appropriate because nothing much is occurring in the movie at this point. Mercifully, Glasser's music is not histrionic, and the piece goes well with the visuals it was chosen to emphasize.

"I'm Going to Kill You" is another quiet cue, probably meant to humanize Benton even as he threatens to kill the three gang members who helped convict him. The movie provides no backstory that allows us to feel any sympathy for him, and it's hard to elicit compassion for someone nicknamed "The Butcher," so the sad and/or romantic library cues that sometimes accentuate Benton do their best to make him seem a little less of a monster.

"Newspaper Headline" is obviously tracked as well, because the orchestral surge at the end occurs almost ten seconds after we see the headline **BUTCHER DIES TODAY**, which it was probably supposed to emphasize, as opposed to the unimportant entrance of Police Capt. Lauder, which the music does stress. While Glasser wasn't necessarily Hollywood's most accurate conductor, not even he could be off by that much! This music again seems to recall Rózsa, and Glasser was proud to admit that he was influenced by other great Hollywood composers such as Max Steiner and Erich Wolfgang Korngold.

When Chasen visits Eva Martin at "The Burlesque House," the Big Band source music provides suitable accompaniment that tries to convince us that the scene is taking place in a hopping joint. The end of the piece comes at the end of the scene, but that doesn't mean it was written for that scene; it just means the music editor lined up the visual and audio endings, then went back to the beginning of the scene and brought the volume in at that point. Although 1:47 of the piece is listed on the cue sheets, just under a minute plays in the movie, implying that either the scene was edited after the music was originally affixed to the film or, more likely, the timing was just made up. This could have been done by Glasser or somebody else, either out of laziness or to help generate some extra royalties: When the movie plays, composers receive royalties proportional to the amount of music they have in the picture.

All of the cues included on *Indestructible Man*'s cue sheets are listed as being "entire," as opposed to "partial," the latter designation being used when a piece of music is not used from beginning to end. While this was sometimes due to editing done after the music was written and recorded for the picture, in the case of *Indestructible Man*, most of the cues were probably edited-down music tracks from earlier films, and hence they should have been listed as "partial." The "entire" designation might have been designed to further prevent anyone from guessing that old recordings were being re-used.

"Backstage" seems to be a few unrelated pieces lumped together under one cue title. The fragments are so different in style that they wouldn't have been written, conducted and recorded as one piece, but rather separately, especially given the completely different orchestrations heard in them which would have required different musicians to play them. The music is heard when Paul enters the burlesque house and goes up to Eva's dressing room, where more source music takes over, this being a wild, brassy swing number. When Eva remembers the envelope Benton gave her, the sad music seems to fit the radio announcement that the Butcher has been executed, and an orchestral surge perfectly accentuates the revelation of the envelope. Despite the match, it's likely this was a well-chosen and well-placed tracked cue rather than an original composition.

If any compositions could have been written specifically for *Indestructible Man*, they would seem to be the three consecutive ones heard during the laboratory sequence where the Butcher is re-animated. "They Bring in the Body," the first of the three compositions, plays as Dr. Bradshaw and his assistant wheel Benton's corpse into the laboratory. The music is often quiet during dialogue passages, which is always helpful, and a couple of cymbal crashes accurately match a pair of quick dissolves—including one showing a blood transfusion. All of this might make one initially think that Glasser wrote this cue to match this particular action, especially as it's rare for a movie to be edited to match a pre-existing piece of music. However, this music is a copy of what was written and recorded by Glasser for the 1951 Rod Amateau-directed Western *The Bushwhackers*, which also featured Chaney. The music's sad, emotional quality would seem to emphasize Benton being dead, although as mentioned earlier, his character did nothing up to this point to elicit any sympathy. Or maybe we're just supposed to feel sorry for him because Chaney's the same actor who portrayed the cursed Lawrence Talbot in *The Wolf Man* and unlucky Dan McCormick in *Man Made Monster*. A more sensible musical approach might have been to capture the action of the scene, or perhaps something befitting a mad scientist's laboratory. But perhaps this music matched the atmosphere being sought better than any other available library tracks.

"Benton Comes Back to Life," the second of the three contiguous pieces, repeats a lot of the music from the previous cue. It builds steadily during the life-giving procedure, the music helping to create suspense despite the flatness of Joe Flynn's lines; Flynn probably needed Tim Conway or Bob Hastings to elicit some enthusiasm from him. Most of the melodramatic musical touches seem to appropriately enhance specific events, such as when an orchestral burst and cymbal match the Butcher returning to life, and surging brass and cymbals highlight him opening his eyes and surveying his surroundings.

There are other music-to-visual matches that occur in the lengthy sequence that again might make one think the cue was written specifically for *Indestructible Man*, but in the climax of *The Bushwhackers* it's heard when Nora (Myrna Dell) shoots the banker (Charles Trowbridge). In *Indestructible Man*, this same orchestral outburst was used to signal Benton returning from the dead. When the banker tumbles to the floor in the Western, well, that music just serves to add drama to *Indestructible Man* as Benton begins to get up. Nobody would notice the mismatches because the general tone of the music matches both sequences so well. Later, when Benton walks lethargically around the laboratory, the music picks up and adds some life to the scene, and that's because in *The Bushwhackers*, it's heard when Nora slips and falls down some steps. The *Bushwhackers* music heard when Nora is shot and dies helps add energy when Benton knocks down the laboratory door, although it does occur a few seconds too early because the filmmakers were stuck with the original recording. When Benton actually breaks down the door, the music is unexpectedly quiet. But this re-use of an older track does show how hard it is to spot a well-chosen piece of tracked music even when there are mismatches to alert one to it. Since so much *Bushwhackers* music appears in *Indestructible Man*, one might wonder why that Western's "Main Title" wasn't re-used in the horror film as well. The most obvious answer is that although it contains some of the same thematic material heard throughout *Indestructible Man*, which would have added some musical unity to the score, it sounds too much like Western music and not at all like horror music.

Glasser, like many other composers of his era, didn't shy away from Mickey-Mousing, a relatively simplistic film scoring approach that matched a visual with a musically corresponding idea, such as somebody climbing a hill while musical notes rise in pitch. Although this sequence manages to synch certain images with some musical moments, this sequence largely avoids obvious Mickey-Mousing.

The third of the three laboratory pieces, "Benton Kills the Doctor," doesn't seem to have too many obvious music-to-visual mismatches on display, and the cue does a relatively good job of accurately reinforcing the action, with cymbal, tympani and blasting brass accentuating Benton murdering Bradshaw and his assistant. Unfortunately, the music seems to consistently lag behind the action by a few seconds, as if it wasn't synched properly to the image. Perhaps if the recording had been moved forward a bit, the piece would have run out before the end of the scene and that's why it was placed where it was. Or perhaps it was a well-chosen library cue just poorly executed by the music spotter or editor. While it's possible it was newly composed for *Indestructible Man*, it's not likely, seeing as the other related cues in this part of the picture were not original. In some more expensive movies, an older piece of music could have been conducted again and newly recorded to specifically try to match these sequences as closely as possible, but if this situation had ever presented itself to Glasser—who loved to compose—it's likely he would have written an original piece rather than re-worked an old one.

As Benton shuffles toward freedom right after the killings, there's a noticeable music edit as the

Music suited to the burlesque house setting is heard when Chasen visits Eva's dressing room, but on their two hamburger drive-in dates, a pleasant love theme plays. Tim Lucas wrote in *Video Watchdog* magazine, "There's a uniquely sweet tone to Adams' wooing of Carr remindful that this film was scripted by two women…, possibly a genre first."

underscore changes dramatically and returns to a recording we've already heard in the picture. Again, the sad quality of the piece is not a very fitting way to personify somebody who has just killed a couple of well-meaning scientists. Unless this was the only suitable recording available for re-use, it seems as if it was felt that poignant underscore would help create sympathy for the mute serial killer.

Although it doesn't seem likely that there was any original music written for *Indestructible Man*, it wouldn't have been out of the ordinary if a few important sequences in a movie—such as the above laboratory scene—featured original compositions while the rest of the film didn't. Sometimes when studios used mostly tracked music in a picture, they would still have some original cues composed for particular scenes that made the movie unique, such as the appearance of a monster or some other memorable character or action. Examples of this are Columbia's *Earth vs. the Flying Saucers* and *20 Million Miles to Earth*, and Universal's *Abbott and Costello Go to Mars* and *Creature from the Black Lagoon*. In these films, some of the music fitting the science fiction portions of the movies was composed by Mischa Bakaleinikoff in the first two and Herman Stein, Henry Mancini, Milton Rosen and Hans J. Salter in one or both of the latter pictures.

"At the Burlesque, #2" plays when Chasen returns to the burlesque house, with another Big Band number being cheaper than having to hire some dancing girls and an orchestra to appear in the movie, to say nothing of patrons in the club. "At the Drive-In" was either meant to be source music playing a pretty melody over a radio, or else it's supposed to serve as Glasser's love theme for Eva and Chasen. The cue features strings, woodwinds and prominent harp, and it helps provide

Sci-fi fans associate Glasser with the genre but, going by the numbers, Western aficionados have an even better claim on him: Glasser worked on dozens of oaters and also the TV series *The Cisco Kid*. Here he is in a latter-day shot with that series' star Duncan Renaldo.

a suitably romantic atmosphere while not distracting too much from the expository dialogue. The library cue ends before the scene is over, so part of it was repeated to fill up the time needed. Glasser was good at writing love themes, as he studied the music of his hero Max Steiner and had learned from the master.

When Lowe offers a job to Joe, the jazzy "In the Bar" is used as source music, probably heard over a radio or juke box. The piece features a combo in addition to some solo piano, making it fairly certain that this composition was written for another picture, or else Glasser probably would have used a prominent piano elsewhere in the score.

An effective cue, "Benton Sees the Car" adds spooky undertones as the Butcher wanders through the hills at night. Low harp emerges from the sparse orchestration, soon giving way to the electronic Theremin, which provides the first sci-fi-horror sound in the movie, almost 27 minutes in. Glasser had quite a bit of experience with the Theremin, orchestrating and conducting Ferde Grofé's 1950 sci-fi score *Rocketship X-M*, and he would later use it generously in 1958's *Earth vs the Spider*. It's not the type of instrument you usually use for subtle orchestral coloring, but rather to be prominent and "in your face" so its otherworldly tone can dominate the scene. If this was an original composition written for *Indestructible Man*, it's likely the Theremin would have been used in both the "Main Title" as well as during the sequence when Benton is brought back to life, as that would have emphasized the main selling point of the picture: that it's a monster movie. Instead, the Theremin only pops up briefly in the film, and in this spot there's nothing particularly out of the ordinary about Chaney lumbering around outdoors. In an original score, that weird instrument would have been perfect to capture the monstrous aspect of "Butcher" Benton; but when he uses his incredible strength to lift Carney's car, some average-sounding orchestral music takes over instead. True, the piece manages to accentuate the visuals and it seems like it could have been written for the movie, but the sound of the music entering and exiting the soundtrack also points to it being another re-used recording.

"Benton Steals the Car" also appears to be mechanically duplicated from an earlier film, as the audio quality is worse than some of the other compositions in the picture. Both it and the following cue, "The Big Roadblock," serve as effective action music highlighting attempts by the police to capture the Butcher. Frenetic brass explodes when Benton insanely attacks everything he sees, although why he gets out of his stolen car to murder some policemen rather than just drive through their feeble roadblock is anybody's guess. The music changes in theme and quality throughout the action, indicating that the recordings used were initially written for different films. This action music would have been just as suitable in a Western, gangster or other genre picture; if you watch and listen to the sequence discerningly, you can tell that the music is high-octane throughout, even when the visuals don't support that kind of accompaniment. Part of this music was used in *The Bushwhackers* when some thugs ride horses into the newspaper office and destroy the place.

"Benton Scares the Girl" contains a number of music edits, as this part of the picture was scored by piecing together fragments of various previously written cues with little effort to do so undetectably. The opening offers relatively subtle accompaniment and quiet orchestration, probably as a compromise between the femininity of Eva and perhaps as another attempt to show the "soft" side of the Butcher. Then

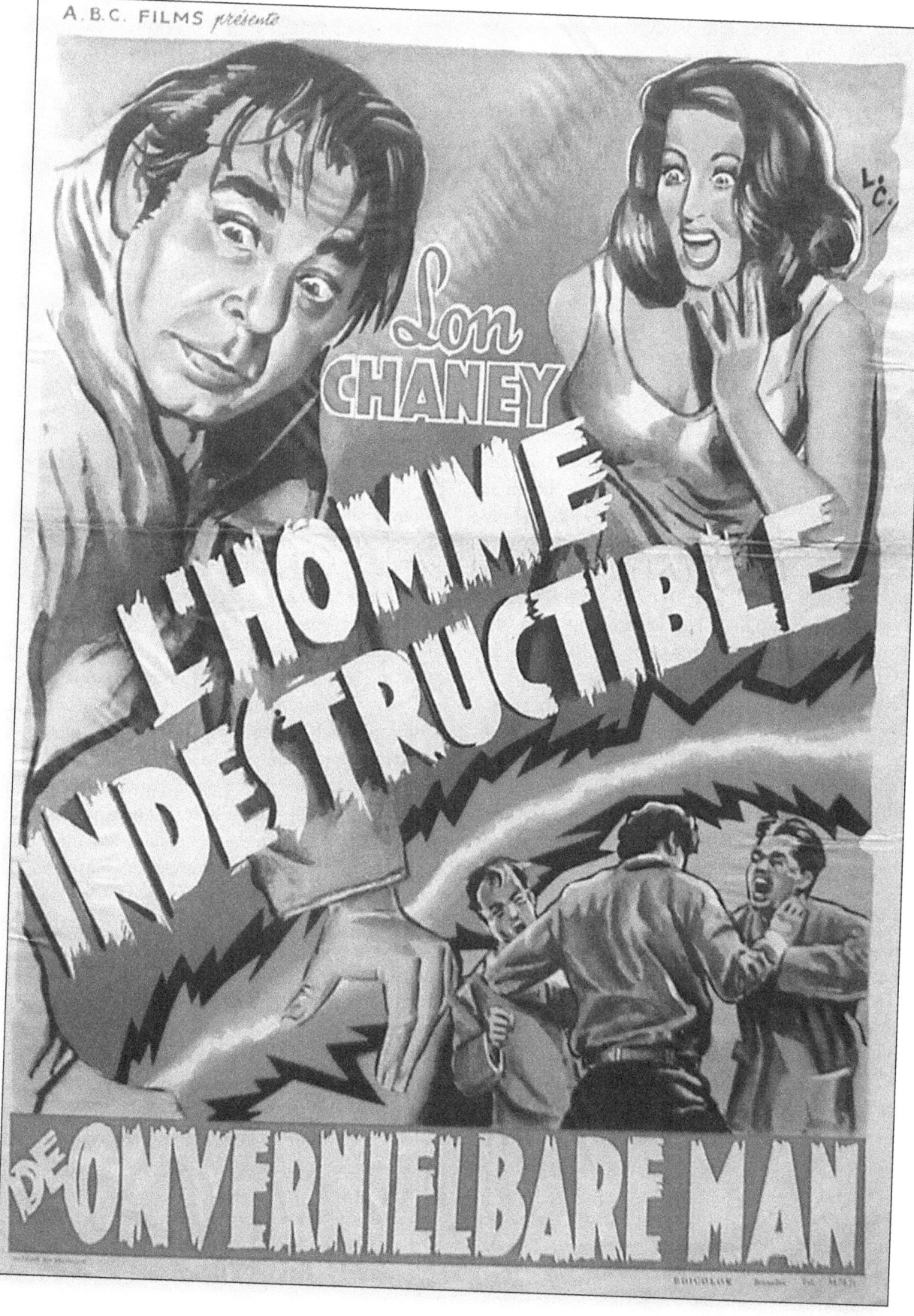

According to the contemporary (1956) *Indestructible Man* review in *Harrison's Reports,* "The manner in which Chaney tracks down the double-crossers one at a time and kills them makes for a number of spine-chilling situations."

again, one has to be careful when reading into why a certain tracked cue was chosen for a particular scene. There are some good matches between music and image, such as when Benton proves his invulnerability by trying to plunge a pair of scissors into his hand. But there are other areas where the music meanders and has nothing to do with the drama, which is what you'd expect given that the cue was composed for another picture and wasn't meant to fit every twist and turn of the new sequence. Much of the footage didn't even need music, such as when Benton exits the burlesque house and Eva phones the police station. This makes one think that very little time and effort was spent on piecing together the soundtrack.

"Benton Kills Again" occurs after a couple of musical snippets that don't appear on the cue sheets. Although the composition itself is rather nondescript, scratchy strings and harp help make this one of the most memorable pieces in the movie, as parts of it stand out orchestrationally from most of the other pieces. After the Butcher arrives outside Joe and Squeamy's apartment and there's a close-up of his fluttering eyes, Theremin makes a quick appearance, but why the electronic instrument was used here, and in such an insignificant fashion, is another mystery. It probably derived from the same film that the earlier Theremin passage was heard in. Harp seems to simulate a clock ticking, perhaps a reminder that Joe's time is quickly running out. Even assuming this is a tracked cue, it's probably not hard finding a library cue that creates tension while also seeming to show the passage of time. The music is particularly moody and effective when Eva rides down Angels Flight, but after a painfully attention-grabbing music edit, the score becomes frantic as the Butcher chases Joe and throws him to his death. The action cue calls too much attention to itself by having a completely different orchestration, and sonically it resembles a fifth-generation print with distorted sound. It's also way too over-the-top for the sequence, and is another re-use of the *Bushwhackers* music heard in the cue "The Big Roadblock." Even after the Butcher walks slowly from a dead policeman, other ancient-sounding music continues at a breakneck pace, oblivious to the lack of action onscreen. Between that and gunshots being heard but not seen, these audio mismatches tend to pull the viewer out of the drama more than usual.

"The Juke Box" in the bar adds some jazzy swing source music when Squeamy worries that Benton has hired someone to kill him. As Benton goes "Into the Office Bldg." to find Squeamy, the soundtrack in fact repeats parts of "Benton Kills Again," which makes some kind of sense since the Butcher is going back to the same location to kill yet another person. The music is prominent in the soundtrack, which is good because there's not too much going on visually, but at the same time the meandering composition fails to build suspense the way it could have it if had been specifically written for the sequence.

When Joe emerges from the elevator and runs into Benton, "Benton Kills the Little Guy" opens with another prominent music edit that introduces more high-gear action music that again sounds like it belongs in a Western. The quality of the recording is fairly substandard, as you can almost hear groove wear from whatever record supplied the library cue. The traditional full-orchestral cues feature shrill brass that cut through the poorly overdubbed screams. The cue name is a bizarre one, and it's entirely possible that whoever pieced together the soundtrack wasn't exactly sure which characters were being killed at what times.

The sad, stringy strains of "The Cops in the Hills" try to elicit audience sympathy for a woman who saw the Butcher snap her boyfriend's back. The cue fits the sequence perfectly, but pretty much any similar-sounding melancholy piece would have done likewise, and it's extremely doubtful Glasser would have composed such a generic piece for this picture. He already had umpteen versions in his past.

"Benton Enters the Sewer" plays as the Butcher descends through a manhole to reclaim the stolen payroll, the music being rather generic and often mixed at so low a volume as to be almost unidentifiable. This was obviously tracked music from an earlier picture, since it would have been ludicrous to have newly composed music written for such an unimportant scene, and the music fades out at the end, what you might expect from the re-use of a previous recording. Unfortunately, the shot of the Butcher walking through the sewer with his hands in his pockets lacks any kind of threat, whereas if Theremin or some other interesting approach had been taken, it might have at least conjured something mysterious to go with the idea of an undead killer lurking beneath the city's streets.

"The Big Chase Begins" highlights the police out in force trying to capture or kill Benton. Fast strings and boisterous brass can't hide the fact that it's just more generic action music suitable for many genres. As Benton listens in on the police from underground, a close-up of his squinting, twitchy eyes again cries out for Theremin or something equally intense, but the music doesn't provide that. Plaintive strings augment the police going down into the sewer, but they aren't dramatically matched to the action, and it's not even the type of music one would normally associate with such a visual.

After the search party splits up, an obvious music edit leads to another previously recorded piece (which goes under the unimaginative cue title "The Chase Continues in the Sewer"), which incongruously creates a feeling of serenity with English horn, other woodwinds, strings and a bit of harp, when a tense and atmospheric musical background was needed. This accompaniment stands out even more for all the wrong reasons when Benton finds the stolen loot, not to mention when the cops close in on him and race down one of the underground passages, a nicely lit and photographed shot that would have been even better with the proper musical accompaniment. It's hard to know what type of scene this piece was originally written for, but probably one in which not much was happening, not the best choice when you're scoring a scene leading up to the climax of a monster movie. While more energetic music might have sounded a bit over-the-top here, it also would have supplied some much-needed energy to the lethargic scenes.

Seen here in a photo from 1975: Composer Glasser apparently liked the high C's.

Although some of the moody music suits the wet underground sewer scenes and maintains a sense of forward motion, other moments make no sense due to the lack of musical expertise used in tracking this portion of the movie, or perhaps the lack of available library music. Glasser's tracked music sometimes swells and then diminishes unrelated to the action on screen, but the composer was occasionally guilty of that even when he wrote original music for a specific scene. There's also yet another repeat of some of the music heard earlier from *The Bushwhackers*, although it sounds more divorced from the action than usual. However, the repetition does create the illusion that there's some thematic approach to the soundtrack. One wishes more library cues featuring Theremin could have been found, as they would have helped make this part of the film a little creepier and more involving.

Further generic action music is heard during "The Flame Thrower." The audio mix is quite awful in this part of the picture, resulting in a cacophonous battle between Glasser's orchestral music and sewer water. One or both of them probably could have had their volume lowered without the film being negatively affected. Movie climaxes have a habit of favoring sound effects over music, so it's a little surprising that Glasser's contribution can be heard as prominently as it is. The sad strings heard when Benton climbs to the surface managed to work in the shot, eliciting some sadness at the fact that the Indestructible Man might not be quite as indestructible as his name suggests. However, the shocking revelation of his disfigured face probably needed some equally horrific sounds in the cue entitled "Benton Is Electrocuted," something Glasser was an expert at composing. The music has a dirge-like quality, which does help let us know that Benton is nearing his end, assuming we had never seen a monster movie before where the monster *always* reaches his end after he's seriously wounded.

The music surges as he begins moving the crane into position and then ascends it, although how he ever learned to operate a crane is thankfully not explained. Crane noise obscures much of the latter part of Glasser's composition, which doesn't really matter since there's not much form to it, but is rather just some melodramatic phrases strung together. The music is almost undetectable as the crane explodes and the Butcher is destroyed. Had Glasser composed the music for this film, one would have understood if he wasn't thrilled with how his musical climax was expurgated, but it's unlikely he even went to see the movie in a theater. He was probably so busy cranking out scores during this part of his career that he didn't get to see too many of his pictures except when he viewed them in order to write the music.

Glasser's "End Title" offers an optimistic ending as Dick receives a much-needed vacation, and he decides to marry Eva without having the courtesy to ask her first. The music seems to be a number of unrelated romantic pieces strung together to fill up the footage. Sometimes a film using tracked music would re-use the "End Title" from the same movie the "Main Title" was taken from, as this would provide a little thematic resolution. However, *Indestructible Man* did not employ the "End Title" from *Philo Vance Returns* as it did that picture's "Main Title." Despite the patchwork quality of the soundtrack, the fact that certain cues from the same movies were re-used multiple times in *Indestructible Man* added a smidgeon of musical continuity to the picture.

By Tom Weaver

⚡ Notice in the small print in *Indestructible Man*'s opening credits that the movie was copyrighted by C.G.K. Productions, Inc., which (according to the movie's music cue sheet) stands for Corwin-Gross-Krasne Productions. It seems completely safe to ass-u-me that Corwin is Sherrill Corwin (1908-1980), who bought *The Man from Planet X* from Wisberg and Pollexfen in 1950 and sold it to UA; and that Gross-Krasne are Jack J. Gross (1902-1964) and Philip N. Krasne (1905-1999), whose company Gross-Krasne produced the TV series *Big Town*, *Mayor of the Town*, *The O. Henry Playhouse et al.*, plus feature films including *Monster from Green Hell* (1957). Gross' quite-impressive fright film résumé from the 1940s includes the memorable Universal Horrors *Captive Wild Woman*, *Phantom of the Opera* and *Son of Dracula* plus the Karloff-Lewtons *Isle of the Dead*, *The Body Snatcher* and *Bedlam*.

⚡ Misspell-a-palooza!: *Indestructible Man*'s opening credits list Mari**on** (should be Mari**an**) Carr[*] and Roy Eng**le** (should be Eng**el**), the latter's name misspelled even though he was something of a regular in Pollexfen's movies, going right back to the start with *Man from Planet X*. Carney's girl is played by Rita Green, according to the credits, but when she turned up in Pollexfen's *Daughter of Dr. Jekyll* she was Rita Green**e**, so one or the other is wrong. Marian Carr's name is correctly spelled on the posters but Ross Elliott here loses the second –t in his surname. The pressbook lists Vy Russell as Vi Russell.

All these victims of screwy spellings got off easy compared to actor Marvin Press, who played the prominent role of Squeamy. In the pressbook, and on every published *Indestructible* castlist in history (until now), the actor is listed as Marvin **Ellis**—the last name of his character Squeamy Ellis accidentally substituted for his own last name, Press!

⚡ In addition to the historic L.A. spots we see in the movie, we are also treated to stock footage of the city's Hall of Justice and San Francisco's San Quentin Prison. Chasen and Eva twice visit a hamburger drive-in that looks like one of Harry Carpenter's Sandwich Stands; the same cars are parked in front both times we see it, days apart story-wise.

⚡ Most ineffectual monster-movie leading man since David Manners?: Casey Adams plays a cop who couldn't find a pair of pajamas in a bowl of soup. Prior to the start of the movie, he spent a year shining the investigative light on the woman he thought was the Butcher's girlfriend before finding out that *she* wasn't his girlfriend, her *roommate* was(!). Throughout the rest, he's on the trail of the Butcher but always about ten steps behind. He even gets lost in the sewer finale.

⚡ In the first burlesque theater dressing room scene, as Chasen (played by Casey Adams) talks with Eva, the voice of a burlesque house worker—Casey Adams' voice—is heard: "You're *on*, Eva!" Eva later

---

[*] It's also spelled Marion Carr in the on-screen credits of her next movie *Kiss Me Deadly*, so perhaps she'd started spelling her name differently.

has a second visitor, Lowe, who enters as a radio newscaster (voice of Adams) reports that the Butcher has just been gassed. Lowe gets to steal the contents of Benton's envelope after Eva is called away by the worker ("Finale, Eva!"), Adams' voice again.

✏ In backstage burlesque house scenes we twice see a showgirl played by an uncredited Dorothy Ford (1922-2010), a former member of Billy Rose's Aquacade and an Earl Carroll showgirl. The 6'3", 38-26-38½" Glamazon had a number of movie roles under her belt; in the 1945 Abbott and Costello vehicle *Here Come the Co-eds* she was part of a female quintet of six-foot-plus pro basketball players, hired to compete against a girls' college basketball team. (The villain who hired these rangy ringers: Lon Chaney!) A&C-wise, she was also the Giant's wife in the comics' *Jack and the Beanstalk* (1952). Ford's advice to other lofty ladies: "If you're tall, be good and tall. Wear high heels: be proud of your height. Build yourself up; don't ever stoop." She lived up to her own advice, wearing four-inch heels when she went out, and in *Indestructible Man* sporting some kind of sky-high headdress. In the mid-1940s, when she was doing some modeling south of the border, she met much-medaled American General Mark Clark, who said of her, "This is the first girl I've ever seen who could go bear hunting armed with a switch."

✏ Twice we see Eva come off the burlesque house stage and both times she's still dressed in her costume. Some burlesque house! The scriptwriters called for something a bit more risqué: They wanted Eva to be shown leaving the stage *carrying* her costume and pulling a robe around her presumably nude self.

"The viewer can't for a moment picture Carr onstage even doing an erotic dance, much less stripping," Ronald L. Smith wrote in *VideoScope* magazine. "In a way, Carr and Adams are like sitcom parents; you wonder what such nice people are doing in a situation like this. Their scenes together have the easy charm of those moments in a movie musical just before the two leads sing to each other."

✏ Before the start of shooting, Sue and Vy met Marian Carr at Western Costume to pick out costumes for her to wear in the movie, and at that point found her to be very friendly. According to Sue, Carr was equally amiable at a point during production when there was a problem with one of those costumes:

I remember—*vividly* remember that she had a tear in the side of one of those short costumes. She wore a real short costume, one of those burlesque deals, and the seam started to come out. Of course we didn't have a wardrobe person working on the show. Jack said to me, "Can you sew it up on her?" I said, "Gosh, I'm terrible at that kind of stuff but, okay, if she's brave enough to let me do it, I'll do it." So I asked her, and she was fine, she laughed about it, and I sewed up the tear on that costume with her *in* it.

✏ YouTube is probably the one place to catch the 1947 Screen Snapshots short *Laguna U.S.A.*, in which we can watch the stars of a Gryphon Players (little theater) production of *Of Mice and Men*—Lon Chaney and Marian Carr among them--cavorting on a Laguna beach.

✏ In the movie, we get several good looks at the burlesque theater's stage door entrance. I assume the eager-beaver black shoeshine man running the stand in that entranceway was the real McCoy and I'd have loved including his name on this book's *Indestructible* castlist. At that stand, according to at least two signs visible in the movie, he provides customers with **THE BEST SHINE IN TOWN – 25¢** but not the most up-to-date reading material in town: When Chasen hops into the chair and picks up a magazine to hide his face from the passing Paul Lowe, it's a *Saturday Evening Post* from January 28, 1950, almost five years old!

In the script, the shoeshiner has a couple lines (see page 51), and his character name is **BOY**.

✏ "Butcher" Benton is reanimated by scientist Dr. Bradshaw—a name quite similar to that of *Indestructible Man* co-writer Sue Brad*ford*. Coincidence? Probably not, because later in the movie we learn that Bradshaw's experiments were tied in with those of a Prof. Dwiggins at Caltech…and Sue's first husband was newspaper and book writer Don Dwiggins. 'Twould appear that Sue had a bit of in-jokey fun naming these characters.

Sue's marriages to Dwiggins *and* d.p. William Bradford both ended in divorce. Another, later husband was assistant director-production manager Wallace Worsley Jr., son of the director of the 1923 *The Hunchback of Notre Dame* and other Lon Chaney movies; they'd met in 1971 on the Georgia set of

Via chemical injection Robert Shayne made himself the Neanderthal Man and via an electrical jolt he created the Indestructible Man. In *Neanderthal* Shayne got top billing for the first and only time in his feature film career, but this was spoiled when his name on-screen was misspelled Robert **Shane**.

Deliverance (Worsley was the film's production supervisor, Sue a secretary). Sue and Wally worked together on a number of subsequent movies, including *E.T. the Extra-Terrestrial* (1982) where Worsley was production manager and Sue production coordinator; they also collaborated on his memoir *Wally Worsley's Half-Century in Hollywood*, published several years after his 1991 death. At age 97, Sue Dwiggins Bradford Worsley died in her Studio City home on New Year's Eve 2011.

⚡ Playing Bradshaw's unnamed assistant is Joe Flynn, future *McHale's Navy* TV star and Disney feature film regular, unbilled in one of his first movies. Another early credit for Flynn was Lippert's *The Big Chase* (1954), which also happened to feature Chaney; in the screen credits of that movie, Flynn was billed Joseph Flynn. Flynn had just turned 30 in November 1954 when *Indestructible* was made. As the assistant, he wears shell-rimmed glasses and a bow tie; he wears them again in the 1956 political drama *The Boss* in order to resemble a young Harry S. Truman (Flynn plays a fictionalized representation of Truman in this movie). *The Boss* provided Flynn with one of his first good movie roles and, probably *not* coincidentally, it was directed by his father-in-law Byron Haskin.

⚡ Once small-screen stardom came Flynn's way, he began guesting on TV talk shows. On a *Merv Griffin* episode he talked about seeing *Indestructible Man* in a theater and noticing that, even though he was playing a serious character, there was some laughter at his delivery of his first lines. And then his *next* lines, and so on. This made him realize that his future might lie not in dramatic acting, but in comedy.

⚡ In July 1974, 49-year-old Flynn went for a solitary nighttime dip in his Beverly Hills pool—and suffered a heart attack in the water. In a way, his comedy movie career (instigated when *Indestructible Man* made

To some fans, *Indestructible Man* is a rip-off of Lon Chaney's first Universal horror vehicle *Man Made Monster* (see photo on left). *Indestructible* poster art that makes the Butcher look as though he's pulsing with electricity (above) may reinforce their attitude.

him aware he wasn't suited for serious roles) had come full circle: That very day he'd finished work on his last movie: Disney's *The Strongest Man in the World* (1975), with Kurt Russell as a college student who becomes unnaturally powerful due to an unforeseen lab mishap (*à la* "Butcher" Benton). *Strongest Man*, of course, was typical light-hearted Disney fare, not any kind of thriller. This was Russell's third time (after *The Computer Wore Tennis Shoes* and *Now You See Him, Now You Don't*) playing the hapless student and Flynn's third as the college's sputtering dean.

⚡ Robert Shayne told me he was blacklisted in the 1950s and yet on his 1950s Hollywood résumé are as many as 50 movies and a mountain of TV episodes, including scores of *Superman*s. I bet hundreds of other 1950s supporting players wished they were as blacklisted!

Shayne had dabbled in life-restoring experiments once before, when he co-starred with John Carradine in *The Face of Marble* (1946). In that Monogram movie, Carradine was the distinguished older scientist and Shayne the not-so-sure assistant—the equivalent of Joe Flynn's *Indestructible Man* character, right down to the bow tie.

⚡ When Benton prowls around the battery storage room adjacent to Bradshaw's lab, notice that when he stops and lays his hands on the edge of a dusty table, he's putting them atop existing handprints in the dust. Chaney must be duplicating his actions from a rehearsal or from a Take One.

Once Benton leaves Bradshaw's lab, which to me looks like a set, it does appear that he's in an actual power station of some kind. Dollars to donuts these interiors (which are part of an electrical station near San Francisco, storywise) and the final reel's power station exteriors (in L.A., storywise) were shot at the same power station. Sue Bradford recalled that the place was in North Hollywood.

⚡ The movie's two hamburger drive-in scenes, in which Monster Kids learn more about the early lives of Chasen and Eva than we probably know about those of our own parents, are "only" about five minutes of the running time, but those minutes pass like hours. Marian Carr wears a different top in the second of these two scenes, but Adams wears the same tie he wore in the first...and in every other scene in the movie, even though it takes place over a period of days. Ross Elliott, Stuart Randall, Ken Terrell and Marvin Press also wear the same clothes from their first scenes to their last.

⚡ The carnival man ("Just call me Carney!") is Eddie Marr, who later played the gruff Sam Arkoff-like studio boss killed by the drooling Teenage Werewolf in

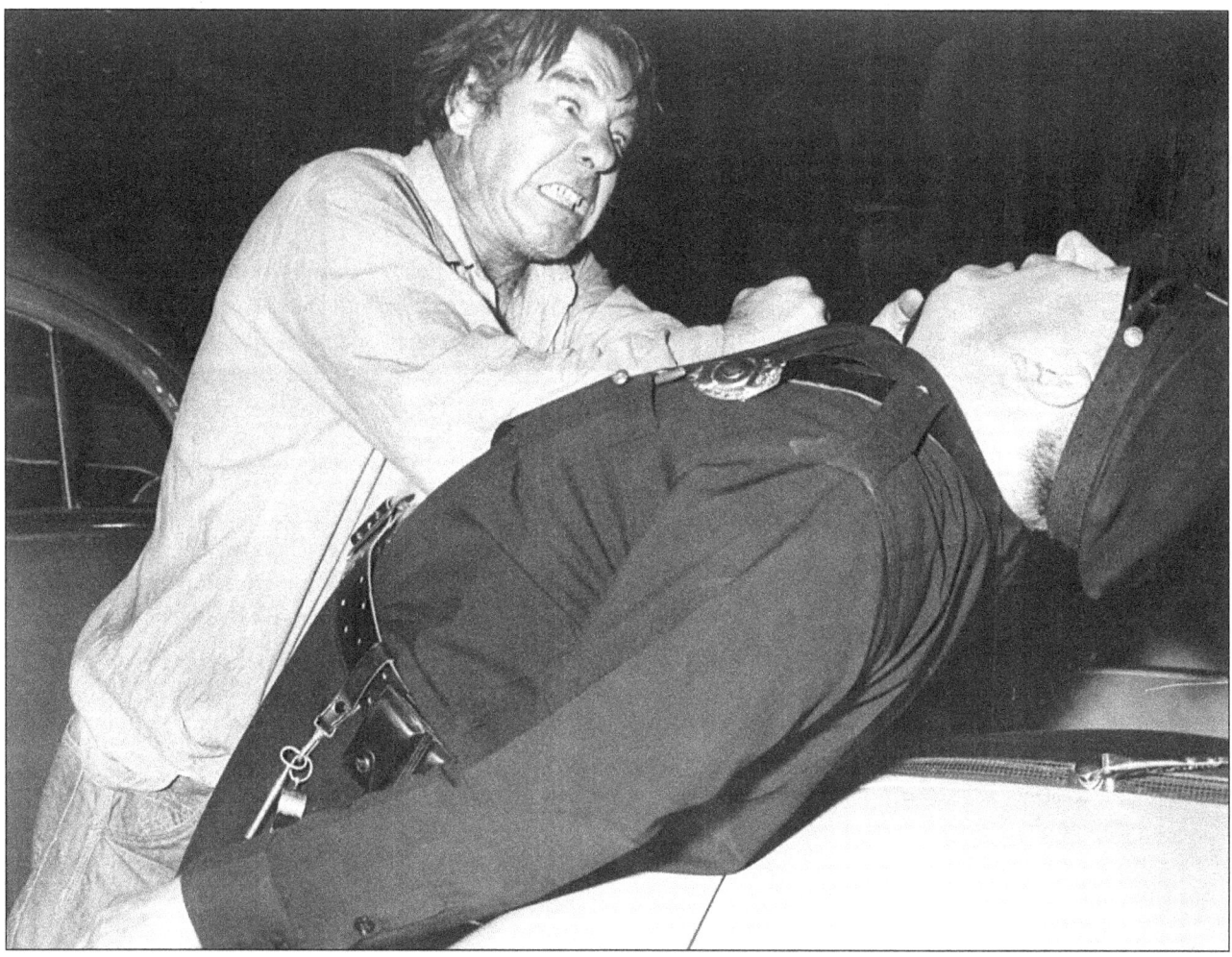

On the basis of *Indestructible Man*'s "excessive brutality" and "suggestive costuming," the Legion of Decency gave it a B rating ("objectionable in part for all"). In this roadblock scene, the "monster-made man" makes a couple of the boys in blue, *black* and blue.

How to Make a Monster (1958). Carney explains their flat tire predicament to Benton and says he has no tire-changing tools, prompting Benton to give Carney's girl (Rita Green) a shove. Notice that as a result, Green knocks heads with Marr. When she takes a moment too long to recuperate she gets a second, no-doubt ad-libbed shove from Chaney.

The Indestructible Man lifts the front end of the car and suddenly Carney *does* have a tool, a tire iron, and somehow he removes the lug nuts from the flat tire, takes it off, puts the spare on and tightens the lug nuts on the spare, with the car suspended in air. Benton should only have lifted the car for the few seconds it would take to remove the flat and replace it with the spare; by holding it up the whole time, he makes things much harder for Carney.

⚡ In the Benton-Carney scene in the script, Benton says something Lennie-ish and Carney makes the disparaging-sounding aside "Some gilhooley!" to the girl. In the movie, it's after Benton has held up the front end of the car long enough for Carney to change the tire that Carney blurts out, "Some gilhooley!" Is this a carnival expression? If you know, visit the forums of the Classic Horror Film Board (monsterkid.com), locate the *Indestructible Man* thread and let *us* know!

⚡ After Benton kills Carney, we see footage of police switchboard operators and dispatchers. This is stock footage from Eagle Lion's *He Walked by Night* (1948), a "*we*-know-whodunit" (before the cops do) about an LAPD manhunt for a cop killer. Seen in the clips are actors Harlan Warde as a police operator, working a switchboard, and Ann Doran as a dispatcher, both reacting to a phoned-in report of the shooting of the police officer. (Starting in 1951, Eagle Lion had begun making its large catalogue of stock footage, sound effects, etc., available.) One wonders if Warde or Doran ever saw *Indestructible Man* and were surprised to find themselves in it.

⚡ In the roadblock scene, Benton climbs out of his car and rushes like a mad bull toward the gun-firing cops. At that point in the story, Benton was taking the word of a stranger, Dr. Bradshaw, that he (Benton) was indestructible, so charging headlong into the cops' line of fire was a pretty ballsy way for him to test out that possibility. But a guy doesn't get an underworld nickname as cool as "The Butcher" doing things by half measures.

⚡ According to the pressbook, Chaney wore a bulletproof vest in scenes where he's "shot" by police handguns and rifles. "[A]lthough the cartridges in the weapons were blank, the blasts knocked him off his feet several times, and his outer clothing was powder burned."

⚡ In the roadblock scene, both of the cops point their guns away from Chaney as they fire so that he won't be hit at close range by the potentially dangerous wadding that come flying out of blank-loaded "movie guns." In 1984, Jon-Erik Hexum, the twentysomething star of a TV series called *Cover Up*, aimed a prop pistol loaded with empty cartridges and gunpowder-filled blanks at his head just for laughs and, with the words "Let's see if I've got one for me," pulled the trigger. R.I.P., you silly goose.

⚡ The woman who screams when Squeamy drops to his death in the Bradbury Building is called a "Woman Attendant" in the script and played by Madge Cleveland, a professional "screamer." According to a 1966 AP article on her career, her then-newest movie *Caprice*—in which she screams at a prowler—was her 83rd such role. The article continues,

> She says there are various types [of screams] for "terror, like when you're about to be murdered; horror, like when a body falls in front of you, and fright, to scare away a prowler."
>
> A perfectionist, she rehearses her screams and learns her lines with a tape recorder—recently in a bean field near her weekend beach home.
>
> But in real life, says Madge, "I'm not the screaming type at all."

In that same year, 1966, Cleveland conferenced with Dell Publishing about a book called *Hollywood Landlady*, based on her experiences with show business tenants in one of her apartment houses. It sounds like it'd be a fun read if she went from screamer to squealer and dished some dirt; I don't know if it was ever written and published.

⚡ The role of burlesque theater performer Francine is essayed by Peggy Maley, a hot-to-trot dame who resembled Lana Turner in her prime. (By this time, Maley was a bit past her "sell-by" date.) Between marriages, and maybe during 'em too, Maley was romantically mixed up with everybody from Artie Shaw and Buddy Rich to Columbia boss Harry Cohn, and from Al Capone's gangster cousin Joe to Egypt's King Farouk.

⚡ Maley's character Francine is just about the only dame who doesn't get "hysterical" in *Indestructible Man*. The Bradbury Building attendant has a hysterical reaction to Squeamy's fatal plunge, a police sergeant calls Eva "hysterical," Chasen describes Carney's girl as "hysterical" and the police sergeant calls Jimmy's girlfriend "hysterical." Vy and Sue could have used Aubrey Wisberg's thesaurus!

⚡ Enjoy the architectural marvels of the Bradbury Building by day…but steer clear at night. The area wasn't the best even back in the 1950s according to actor Ewing Brown, part of the cast of the 1951 version of *M*. He told me,

> We were shooting downtown in the old Bradbury Building, a very ornate place with birdcage elevators and everything in it, built in the 1890s. We were shooting in a parking lot within the building, working from 10 or 11 o'clock at night to six in the morning. That's a pretty spooky neighborhood at night—desolate, nothing there, nobody on the street except people breaking into buildings.
>
> Raymond Burr and I were supposed to make this rush-in entrance, coming in from an alley in the back of the building. It was pitch dark in the alley as Ray and I were standing outside waiting for our cue, and Ray stepped back in the dark and stepped on something. "What the hell's *that*?" he asked. I flicked my cigarette lighter on, and there was a guy lying face up, eyes open blood comin' out of the mouth, with a knife—I mean, a biiiig butcher knife—stuck in his chest! Ray let out a scream, and *jumped*, and the cigarette lighter went out, and there we

In the 1930s and '40s, Republic's stunt regulars were the best in the business, and Ken Terrell was a member of that daredevil dream team. He was seen in many of the studio's serials, often playing more than one part in each. In this series of photos, Terrell is manhandled by Captain America in Chapter 6 of Republic's same-name 1944 serial.

were, the two of us, alone in the dark with this dead or dying guy at our feet! We went through the door and yelled, "Somebody call the police! Help!" Turns out the guy was dead. Well, now Ray was *not* going out into the alley again without police protection!

⚡ As Eva is waiting at the Angels Flight boarding station, notice in the background the sign listing the price of two rides as five cents and the price of a 30-ride book as 50 cents.

⚡ It's strange to see Ken Terrell on crutches for his role of Joe Marcelli because in real life Terrell was a highly acrobatic stuntman. In 1922, this native of Georgia was a teenage entrant in the World's Most Perfectly Developed Man contest, which was won by Charles Atlas. Then, in vaudeville houses here and abroad, he had a popular knockabout act in which he was paired with two other future Hollywood stunt people, Jimmy Fawcett and Fawcett's wife Helen Thurston. His Hollywood stunt career began in the mid-1930s.

In the July-August 1999 issue of *Western Clippings* magazine, Neil Summers (a stuntman himself) devoted his column to Terrell, revealing that according to Terrell's personal files, "he appeared in and completed 1354 stunts, including fights, knife and sword fights, Jiu Jitsu, car chases, skids, crashes, leaps and transfers to and from cars and trucks, high dives, long swims, high falls, bulldogs and anything else the script called for." In the 1950s Terrell's ferret face became familiar to monster movie fans as he made appearances in Pollexfen's *Indestructible Man* and *Port Sinister* plus 1958's *The Brain from Planet Arous* (as the trigger-happy general zapped by John Agar's deadly stare) and *Attack of the 50 Foot Woman* (as the battling butler). He also stunt-doubled Arthur Shields as Mr. Hyde in *Daughter of Dr. Jekyll* and one of the scientists dumped out of the upended dinghy by the Gill Man in *The Creature Walks Among Us* (1956).

Unfortunately for Terrell, in 1958 he badly broke his leg or foot (sources differ) while rehearsing for a Chevrolet commercial and this made it impossible for him to return to full-time stunt work. One stunt assignment during this fallow period was a short fight with fellow stunter Eddie Parker on a Jack Benny TV episode—with the 59-year-old Parker suffering a fatal heart attack right afterwards!

Terrell's health deteriorated, his marriage broke up, he felt forgotten and, according to Summers, "he died alone on March 8, 1966."

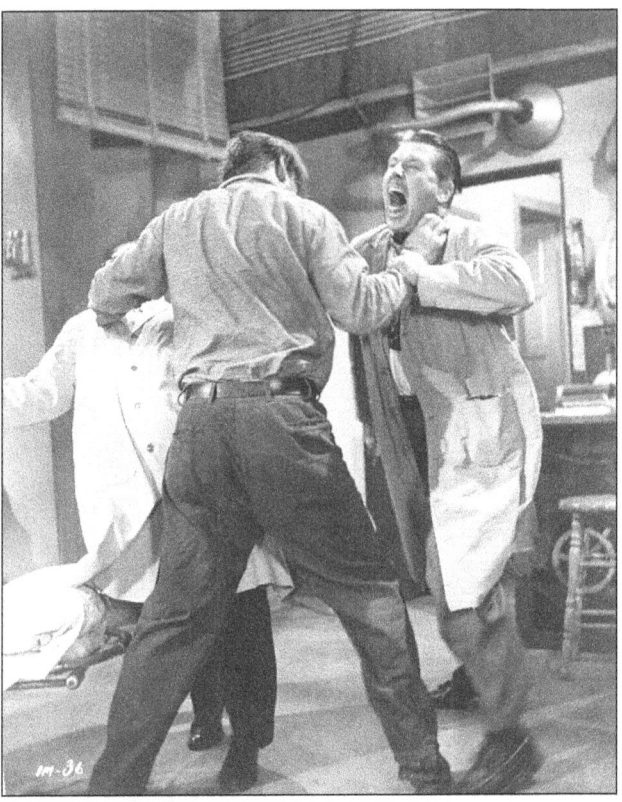

Scientist Shayne and assistant Flynn give the executed "Butcher" (Chaney) the gift of life; here's their receipt, a strangulation that looks like the set-up for a pro wrestling double choke slam. For the now indestructible Benton, this is just the tip of the not-so-niceberg.

⚡ Benton has just thrown Joe down the concrete utility stairway behind the Hillcrest (from Olive Street all the way to Clay Street—quite a throw!) when a police car pulls up on Olive. The cop riding shotgun gets out, confronts Benton and shoots twice. We hear the first shot while we can see the gun, and there's no flash or smoke. Chaney's between the camera and the gun when we hear a second shot but again we see no smoke. Sound-effects-only gunshots are a cheat and it spoils the scene. Maybe Chaney didn't want blanks fired at him at such close range—or perhaps Pollexfen & Co. were working on that location without permits and didn't want to attract attention. The reason will remain a mystery.

So will the mystery of why the cop's partner dropped him off in front of mad dog killer Benton, and then abandoned him there!

⚡ The Clay Street foot of that long staircase was also seen in *Once a Thief...*, a 1950 melodrama with a bespectacled Chaney in fourth-billed support.

A vintage shot of Pollexfen, the man who gave Monster Kids the gift of *Indestructible Man*. During his lifetime, his friend Vy Russell described him to me as "obviously a character, but a *delightful* person and a very bright man. The mind works much faster than the talk—he stutters a bit—but he's very knowledgeable in all areas. And what he doesn't know, he has a fertile-enough imagination that he can make up for it [*laughs*]! I know he wrote articles on how to build a swimming pool, for instance—the most unlikely thing in the world! But he becomes an authority at the drop of a hat."

⚡ Within a few weeks or perhaps even *days* of the *Indestructible* invasion of the Bunker Hill area, moviemakers were again at the site: director Robert Aldrich and star Ralph Meeker, shooting a scene for the Mike Hammer movie *Kiss Me Deadly* (1955). With Angels Flight in the background, Meeker drives his Corvette roadster on Clay Street, parks it at the bottom of the staircase and begins scaling the steps. Soon we see him in front of the Hillcrest Hotel where Chaney, Marian Carr and Ken Terrell had enacted some *Indestructible* scenes.

Pollexfen with a fish he claimed to have caught off Carmel. Wife Lee cast doubt on his "fish story."

⚡ The movie is full of moments of violence: the two-for-one strangulation of Bradshaw and his assistant, Carney fatally kicked face-first into the ground, the Butcher standing up to rifle and pistol fire, screaming cripple Joe Marcelli gorilla-pressed and hurled down a cement staircase, screamy Squeamy dropped five stories into the Bradbury Building lobby, the skin blistering off of Benton's face as the flame thrower is deployed, etc. But when I tried to "congratulate" Vy and Sue on writing a script filled with such brutal touches, Vy pointed to the individual actually responsible: "Oh, Pollexfen just *drooled* over things like that!" she laughed. "The gorier, the better, if he could get by with it. And, in all fairness, that sort of thing makes money, it shocks the public and draws them in."

But Pollexfen didn't think the violence in this movie was particularly "extreme." "Much of it was handled by cuts, suggestions, sound effects," he wrote me. "Of course, when you're dealing with an indestructible man, there's bound to be quite a bit of destruction."

⚡ On September 9, 1983, Pollexfen sent me a long letter, the first page outlining how he got into the movie business. I whittled that part of it down to just a few sentences for the intro to my Pollexfen interview in *Fangoria* #35 (April 1984), and the rest of it went to waste for over 30 years. Here's the full account in Pollexfen's own words:

> I was born in San Diego in 1908, but was raised mostly in Mill Valley, California. My family moved to Los Angeles toward the end of grammar school days. History was always my best school subject, and is still a major reading interest. Was a fairly steady moviegoer through school, but newspapers were the big fascination, career-wise. Following school, I started in the mode as a copyboy on the old *L.A. Express*. With a brief time out at L.A. City College, I worked on a batch of other dailies as a reporter and feature writer—plus handling a few non-movie publicity jobs, and writing and producing three plays of the type that could be classified as off-Broadway today—a long way off.
>
> I drifted into doing magazine articles. I must have written hundreds, hitting markets from *Collier's* to the trades. A little fiction, but generally I stuck to articles.
>
> MGM was intrigued by an article I had done, "Nelly Bly," and offered me a contract—and so I was in [the] movie business. By this time it was close to the end of 1940. I finished the script at Metro and Universal hired me for *Mister Big* [1943]. Halfway through the script my draft number came up. I finished the last half of the script in a weekend, and the next four years I was an Air Force non-com, sitting at a typewriter knocking out training films and manuals.

At this point in the letter, he began to describe writing screenplays in collaboration with Aubrey Wisberg.

⚡ Vy may have *written* sci-fi movies—*Indestructible Man* and *Monstrosity*—but don't make the mistake of thinking this means she *liked* sci-fi movies. "Not at all!" she told me. "No, but you write what the market offers. …I wouldn't go see a movie that was sci-fi. Sorry about that, because I know *you* have a warm spot in your heart for that stuff. I hadn't seen any of those movies, I don't think." Sue on the other hand grew up reading H.G. Wells and other such authors, and was a Trekkie. In later years, Vy's son Mike introduced Sue to the writings of Kurt Vonnegut.

⚡ Best line in the movie? I get the impression that Bradshaw's assistant's (Joe Flynn) incredulous "You mean you're going to give him 287,000 volts?" would get a lot of volts—er, *votes* from Monster Kids, but I've got my own favorites:

- In the bar, the woman lush reacts to the entrance of Joe Marcelli on crutches: "I've seen 'em stagger on two legs, but he's doin' it on four!"

- Later in the same scene, Paul Lowe's disgusted comment to Old Smuggler-craving yegg Marcelli: "You used to be the best torch man in town. Now I don't think you could crack a safe if you knew the combination!"

- But I have to give the top prize to another Lowe line: In San Quentin, he reacts to a death threat from the hours-from-execution "Butcher" Benton by blowing him a kiss (or maybe it just looks like he does) and cheerfully chirping, "So long, dead man!" The walk-off is what sells it.

⚡ Most memorable shots in the movie: the insert closeups of Chaney with his rheumy eyes twitching. They interrupt the action while he's contemplating revenge in the power station basement; while looking at Carney's girl; while shaking Eva in her dressing room; while standing outside the window of Squeamy's apartment; and *twice* while evading cops in the sewer. In some of them, he looks so hirsute with his mane of hair and big sideburns that you'd think he was starting a werewolf transformation. Continuity-wise these shots are a disaster: Sometimes the backgrounds don't match the backgrounds in the before and after shots, and his facial expressions and sometimes his hair are also different than in the surrounding shots. These whacked-out inserts were somebody's idea of a good idea and let's give that devil his due: Fans of the movie are still enjoying them and talking about them 60 years later, so apparently it *was* a good idea.

⚡ When you get to the part of the *Indestructible Man* script where the Butcher takes his gal Eva to the cave and stands off the police (a scene shot but

The concept of truth in advertising is butchered by *Indestructible Man* posters that depict action tableaus nothing like we find in the movie.

drains built to siphon off the flash floods of the rainy season. Many of the tunnels are large enough for two cars to drive abreast. Here were 700 miles of hidden highway…" Possibly some of the shadowy figures we see at a distance in *Indestructible Man*'s subterranean scenes are that movie's stars Basehart, Scott Brady and Roy Roberts.

⚡ Chaney famously enjoyed doing as many of his own action scenes as he could*, but there might be one *Indestructible Man* shot where he has a double: In the sewer, when the bazooka blast hits the Butcher in the stomach (a big flash powder explosion), it doesn't look like Chaney to me.

⚡ As Benton is being hit by the flame thrower, he looks more burned every time we glimpse his face amidst the fire. This is reminiscent of the lab-fire finale of *The Ghost of Frankenstein* (1942) in which the face of the Monster is more burned and blistered from one shot to the next. Benton must also be wearing indestructible shirt and pants because, other than a few holes and shortened shirt sleeves, they're in better shape than *he* is when, at the end of the bazooka-bullet-fire barrage, he exits the sewer through a power station manhole. Notice, however, that by the end of the power station scene, there are more and much bigger holes in his clothes than at the beginning.

⚡ It never occurred to me to ask any of my *Indestructible* interviewees who created the burn-face makeup on Chaney in the final minutes of the movie, or how it was done. In the *Indestructible Man* pressbook (reprinted in the back of this book), one item says that Chaney was his own makeup artist for the scene, designing the makeup in "a theatrical dressing room" he'd set up in his North Hollywood home. Could be.

With all participants now deceased, we're forced to speculate about how the makeup was done—and who better for that job than Michael F. Blake, Emmy-winning makeup artist and author of three top-notch books about Chaney's "Man of a Thousand Faces" father? Michael cast his experienced eye on the Butcher's cremated kisser and opined,

> Since *Indestructible Man* was a very low-budget independent movie, they probably would not

then scrapped), you can't help but think of the nearly identical situation in *The Neanderthal Man* where the monster takes *his* gal Ruth (Doris Merrick) to the cave and stands off the posse members. In *Neanderthal* the posse men even talk about driving him out with tear gas; Chasen uses tear gas on Benton in this script's cave scene.

⚡ If you like the atmospheric way some of the sewer shots were photographed, you have cinematography great John Alton to thank: It's more stock footage from *He Walked by Night*, the tale of an L.A. manhunt for a cop killer, photographed by Alton. Like Indestructible Man Benton, that movie's cop killer (Richard Basehart) also hides out under the streets of the city; as that film's narrator Reed Hadley puts it, this killer "had discovered an ideal avenue of escape. Under Los Angeles is a vast and intricate system of huge storm

---

*"I always work out my screen fight routines. I really like to do them," he told an interviewer around the time he made *Captain China* (1950). "If somebody else maps out the action, the rough stuff is liable to be soft-pedaled for fear of maiming the actors. That ruins a movie fight."

have had access to a makeup lab to create a burned face via foam appliance. Instead, the film's makeup artist would have had to "pull something out of his case" (which is makeup terminology for "pulling a rabbit out of your hat").

The most likely way the burned makeup was accomplished was by using liquid latex and Kleenex (or latex and cotton).

After painting sections of Lon Chaney's face with liquid latex, the makeup artist would then apply sections of Kleenex or cotton, pressing them into the latex. Once the face was covered, the makeup artist would paint additional coats of latex, drying each coat before another application.

In some cases, makeup artists used spirit gum in place of the latex. Still in use today, spirit gum is an adhesive to apply beards and such. Back in 1956 it would have been the strongest adhesive available. However, with someone like Lon Jr. who liked to drink, if he sweated (and he likely did), the alcohol in his system would mix with the sweat, which would break down the spirit gum. (Alcohol is one remover we use to take off spirit gum.)

The latex-Kleenex (or latex-cotton) combo can be painted with a castor oil base we called Rubber Mask Grease. (A regular makeup base would go ashen against the rubber.) Once it is heavily powdered, it is camera-ready.

⚡ Unusual amongst old movies with human monsters, *Indestructible Man* allows its title character to commit suicide in the finale: He climbs up into the electrical works, purposely puts the machinery into operation, then climbs to the top and waits for the one-two punch of high voltage and explosion. This, of course, was not the moviemakers' original intent: In the script, Benton's up there trying to kill Chasen, but the wily cop turns the tables and destroys him.

⚡ According to Burl Lampert, who had the fun opportunity to repeatedly watch *Indestructible Man* with live Jack Pollexfen "commentary," Pollexfen said it was "a great shoot," one of the few that he really liked. "Jack was quite proud of it," Lampert adds. "'Made money,' he'd say with half a smile. It really was one of his faves."

⚡ The pressbook describes Casey Adams as a specialist in playing "parboiled lawmen." Since "parboil" means to half-cook a piece of food, one suspects they meant to call him *hard*-boiled. The same pressbook item says that the electrical charge that ultimately kills the not-quite-indestructible man was seven million volts.

Another pressbook story reminds us that Chaney is carrying on the tradition of his famous dad, who so memorably portrayed "the humpback dwarf" [*sic*] in the silent *Phantom of the Opera*.

⚡ Distributor Allied Artists most frequently double-billed *Indestructible Man* with *Invasion of the Body Snatchers*, the sci-fi classic which, in an early 1957 *Variety*, was included in the newspaper's long list of the "Top Money Films" (domestically) of 1956. Assuming that most of the folks who saw *Body Snatchers* on a twin-bill with *Indestructible Man* stuck around for the latter, that would make the Chaney vehicle one of the most widely seen sci-fi-horror flicks in its weight class in 1956. This book's research associate Dr. Robert J. Kiss points out, "I can't help thinking that most of the box office takings reported (high when co-billed with *Invasion of the Body Snatchers*, low when billed alongside *World Without End*) tell us more about the pulling power of the main feature, while adding to the sense of *Indestructible Man* as a near-irrelevance on the bill!"

Reviewer Alan Kass of the newspaper *The Florida Flambeau* wrote (March 26, 1957) that *Body Snatchers* was "a fairly good and exciting chiller," then added, "It is unfortunately teamed up with something like *The* [*sic*] *Indestructible Man*."

⚡ Indestructible Fans sometimes liken the movie to *Man Made Monster* on the rather slim basis of an electric jolt turning Chaney into a super-powered killer, but the movie to compare it to is actually the *Most Dangerous Man Alive* (1961). Check off the similarities: En route to the gas chamber (check) at San Quentin (check), a convicted killer (check) escapes into a remote area where a new type of bomb is about to be tested. Exposed to the mutating rays of Cobalt Element X, his body becomes like steel (check). He assaults a vehicle owner and steals the guy's wheels (check, check) in order to get back to the city (check) and then begins tracking down and killing criminal confederates who had betrayed him (check, check); he also visits an old gal-pal (check). He slays several of his former confederates, two by making them fall to their deaths (check), but the police finally track him down (check) and unleash a flame thrower squad on him (check).

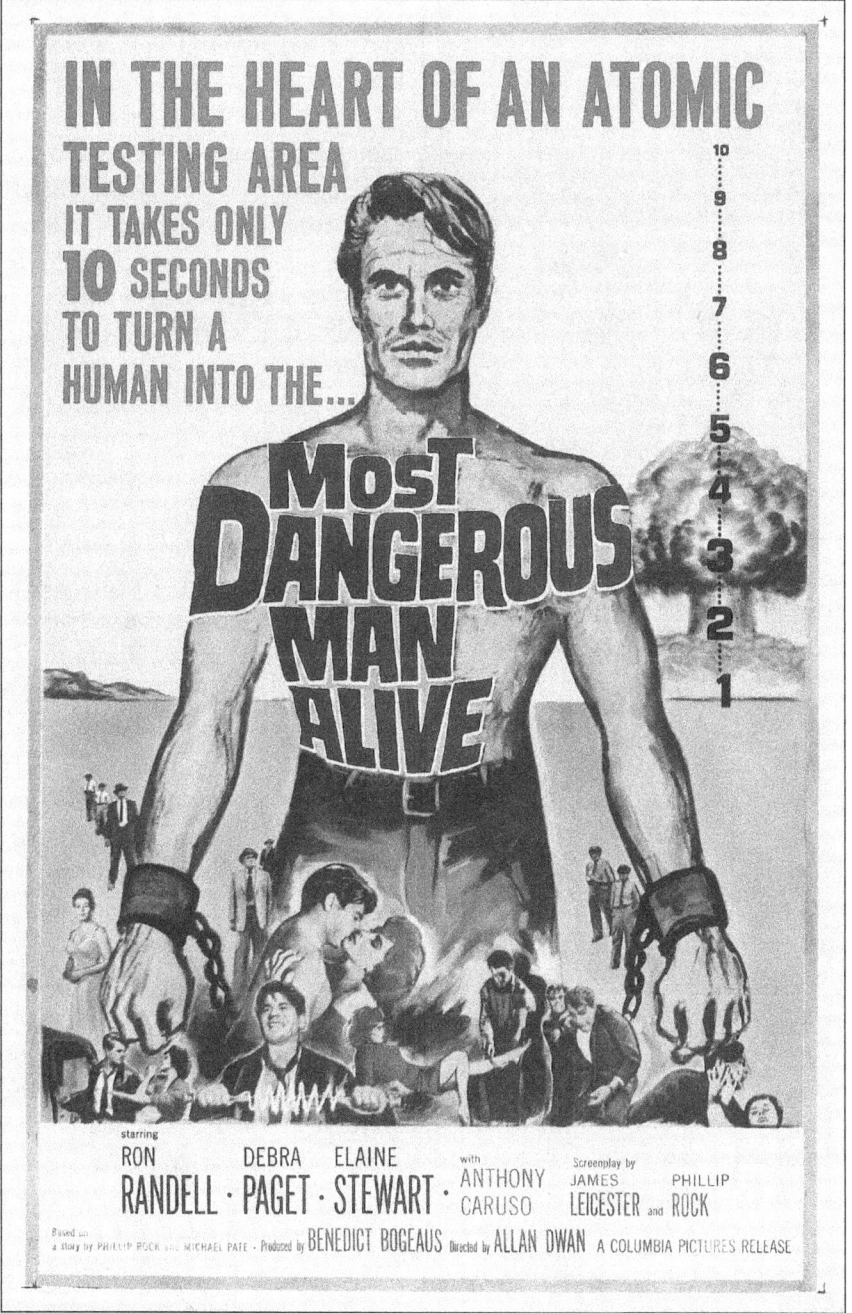

Most Derivative Man Alive?: Made in Mexico in the spring of 1960, this Ron Randell-starring SF-gangster melodrama is so similar to *Indestructible Man* that it's hard to believe that no one involved saw the older picture.

large secret lab behind his spooky wax museum. In this outlandish horror-comedy, however, Lon isn't playing a garden-variety restored-to-life guy but a thousands-years-dead mummy. And not a garden-variety thousand-years-dead mummy, but one who transforms into a werewolf by the light of the full moon! Yes, the actor reprises *two* of his Universal monsters in the same movie—although as the mummy, he does nothing but stand or lie around dead. Once he's resuscitated and cleaned up, he's dressed in 20th-century clothes, including a dark shirt that makes it obvious that *some*one (maybe Chaney) remembered Chaney's wardrobe from his old Wolf Man series.

It's also obvious that someone remembered *Abbott and Costello Meet Frankenstein* (1948) because the plot soon involves the scientist's determination to transplant the brain of a comically lazy night watchman (Tin Tan) into the monster. Chaney fans will wonder how often it's really him under all the werewolf hair, especially when the werewolf is running alongside cars on a nighttime highway, climbing the side of a building while carrying a girl, etc. A good bit of the story is played straight and, partly because Chaney's in the cast, it's actually quite watchable.

James Leicester and Phillip Rock based their screenplay on the story "The Steel Monster" by Rock, actor Michael Pate and, uncredited, actor Leo Gordon. *Most Dangerous Man Alive* probably cost two or three times what *Indestructible Man* did, but doesn't have a fraction of its cut-rate, cockeyed charm.

The Mexican-made *La Casa del Terror* (1960) finds Chaney again playing a character restored to life, this time by a ruthless scientist (Yerye Beirute) with a

It's Chaney who uses electricity to bring life to a dead man in the rock-bottom *Dr. Terror's Gallery of Horrors* (1967), an anthology horror flick shot in five days and comprised of five stories, each more gloriously goofy than the one before. Batting fourth in the lineup is the ten-minute "Spark of Life," set in Scotland in the mid-1800s although no one affects a Scottish accent, and a then-modern sink and telephone are seen. Chaney, a medical school lecturer, theorizes that life can be returned to the dead via electricity; but when two of his students say they want to try to resurrect

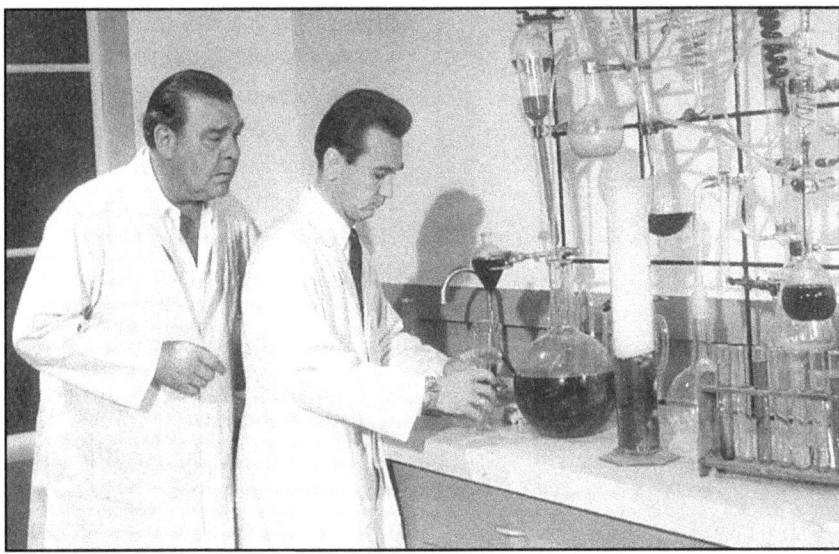

If you thought the *Indestructible Man* laboratory left something to be desired, check out the shoddy set on which Chaney and Ron Doyle conduct their life-restoring experiment in *Dr. Terror's Gallery of Horrors.*

a medical cadaver, a suddenly aghast and angry Chaney snaps, "*What* did you say? How did you *think* of such a thing?"—the doctor apparently forgetting that they're offering him the chance to test *his* own theories (which he'd just finished discussing)! The electrobiological experiment is a success but it turns out that the resuscitated fellow is a three-time knife murderer, and there's a "surprise" ending that you can see coming from halfway to Edinburgh. Funniest moment in the movie: The dead man pops up and Chaney, never hammier, exults, "I'm a genius! Do you know that I'm a genius? Ha ha ha ha haaaaaa!" as he scampers off-camera like an over-stimulated kid. Even when Chaney plays a scientist, Lennie creeps in. It was the actor's last speaking role in a horror film.

⚡ For Chaney fans who can't get enough of a good thing (Lon behind bars swearing revenge), the *Studio 57* episode "The Ballad of Jubal Pickett" (1956) sounds like a good companion piece for *Indestructible Man* with its tale of Jubal, a giant of a convicted killer (Chaney) who vows to escape and wreak vengeance on his own brother (Keenan Wynn) who turned him over to the law. A switch on *Indestructible Man*: Jubal and a couple confederates try to rob a bank *after* his escape, while he's en route to Wynn's. According to *Variety*, Tex Ritter intermittently sings the title ballad, which must give the tale a *High Noon* (1952) flavor.

"Gunfire" (1962), an episode of *The Rifleman*, takes place entirely in the inky darkness of one long night. Chaney plays outlaw Charlie Gordo, a prisoner in Marshal Micah's (Paul Fix) jail, and with supreme confidence he says that he'll kill anyone who tries to take him to Yuma Prison for his scheduled hanging. Once Gordo's trio of gang members begin striking out of the shadows, Micah's deputies let him down, making Micah the *High Noon*-Gary Cooper equivalent in this story. Directed by Richard Donner, it's a grim, ominous and quite violent 30 minutes and, like "Jubal Pickett," a treat for fans of Chaney in "Butcher" Benton-like roles.

Indestructible Man's Ross Elliott is in both episodes, in "Jubal Pickett" as a reporter who sees the story come to a twist ending, in "Gunfire" as a deputy whose fear of Gordo and his gang prompts him to turn in his deputy's badge.

⚡ When Allied Artists released their '50s horror flicks to TV, the ones with "awkward" running times (too long to run in a 60-minute slot, too short to run in a 90) were *stret-t-t-c-c-c-h-h-hed* out by Hollywood director-editor Herbert L. Strock. Courtesy of "Doc" Strock, in each of these movies a lengthy written foreword scrolled up the screen ever so slowly; many frames were duplicated in non-dialogue shots, giving all movement a jerky slow-motion look; shots from within the movie were run twice; a scrolling castlist was added at the end; and a scene from within the movie now did double-duty, starting the show as a pre-credits sequence! For *Indestructible Man*, the Butcher's resuscitation scene became the pre-credits sequence, and five shots from the sewer finale were replayed, flipped right for left to camouflage the repetition.

When *Indestructible Man* was released on tape by Allied Artists in the early days of home video, the print was the movie's TV version.

⚡ Indestructible Fans who saw the TV version umpteen times as kids may remember part or all of its written-for-TV foreword:

The journeys of Jules Verne and H.G. Wells into the impossible, have suddenly become real! Frankenstein's fantastic dissecting of vital organs for use in another body, is actually happening! Yesterday's Science-Fiction is Today's Fact!

What would occur if a biochemist succeeded in splitting human cells, causing them to multiply like the atom? .. Could the flesh be changed? Could a robot be made from a man?

COME with us, while we explore the possibilities! We start with a man about to die...

⚡ According to writer-producer-director Fred Olen Ray (who penned the introduction to this book), he'd always wanted to do a loose remake of *Indestructible Man* because he was so fond of the film and its simple storyline. "When I started working with Aldo Ray," he told me, "I got even more interested because I felt that he mirrored Chaney in some ways. He was a big, tough guy who wrestled with the bottle a bit and it affected his work at times." He continued,

> We had just spent $10,000 building a laboratory set for some new scenes on *Deep Space* [1988] and after we shot a day on them they were to be destroyed. It really was a pretty cool set and I kept wondering how I could make some use of it before it was torn down. Aldo was in town for a day and it occurred to me that we could possibly shoot the opening scene for this new film with him and maybe finish it up later. Aldo was game and I quickly wrote the script.
>
> Richard Harrison, Jay Richardson and Dawn Wildsmith came in and we shot a scene where Aldo is a criminal headed to Death Row who agrees to an experiment. If he survives, he walks away a free man. If he doesn't, well, he was headed for the chair anyway. I shot three lab scenes, about ten minutes. The concept for the rest of the movie was that he gets fried and is taken away in a morgue wagon, but revives in transit and escapes. His face is disfigured and he dons a mask and goes on a killing spree to take revenge on the gangsters that ratted him out. I always figured that [because of the mask] we could complete the film later without Aldo if he flaked, which he was prone to do, using a double. He died before we got any further. At the time we called it *Beyond Fear* and even ran an ad in *Variety* for it. I later put the edited 35mm workprint on the DVD of *Terminal Force*, a Richard Harrison double feature from Retromedia.

A heavily made-up Chaney was in the Gary Cooper Western *High Noon* (1952) as a retired marshal who, like all the other men in town, hasn't the courage to help Cooper stand up to the trio of killers heading their way. In an episode of TV's *The Rifleman*, it's a trio of killers coming to North Fork to rescue the jailed Charlie Gordo (Chaney) that has the town's lawmen in a sweat.

⚡ Science hasn't yet figured out *why*, but if you see *Indestructible Man* the first time or two as a kid, the names "Paul Lowe, Squeamy Ellis and Joe Marcelli" get stuck in your brain for the rest of your life.

The movie was banned in Germany for exhibition on "Holy Days" and just plain banned in Indonesia. Other movies banned in that Southeast Asian country at around that same time included *Dial M for Murder*, *1984*, *A Kiss Before Dying*, *Man in the Vault*, *The Black Sleep* and *Pharaoh's Curse*.

Speaking of censorship, the PCA's Geoffrey Shurlock was sent the script before shooting began, and a few lines caught his eye:

• In an Eva-Chasen dressing room scene that didn't make it into the movie, Chasen talks about his failure to locate the stolen payroll and says forcefully, "That $600,000 damn near cost me my job."

• After the Bradbury Building killing of Squeamy, Capt. Lauder hears from witnesses that the killer was bulletproof and bitterly says to Chasen, "**God help us** when this hits the papers."

• Later in the movie, Lauder gets fed up with their slow progress in catching Benton and barks at Chasen, "Damn it all, man—the Chief's on my neck—the Commissioners're on his and the Mayor's on theirs."

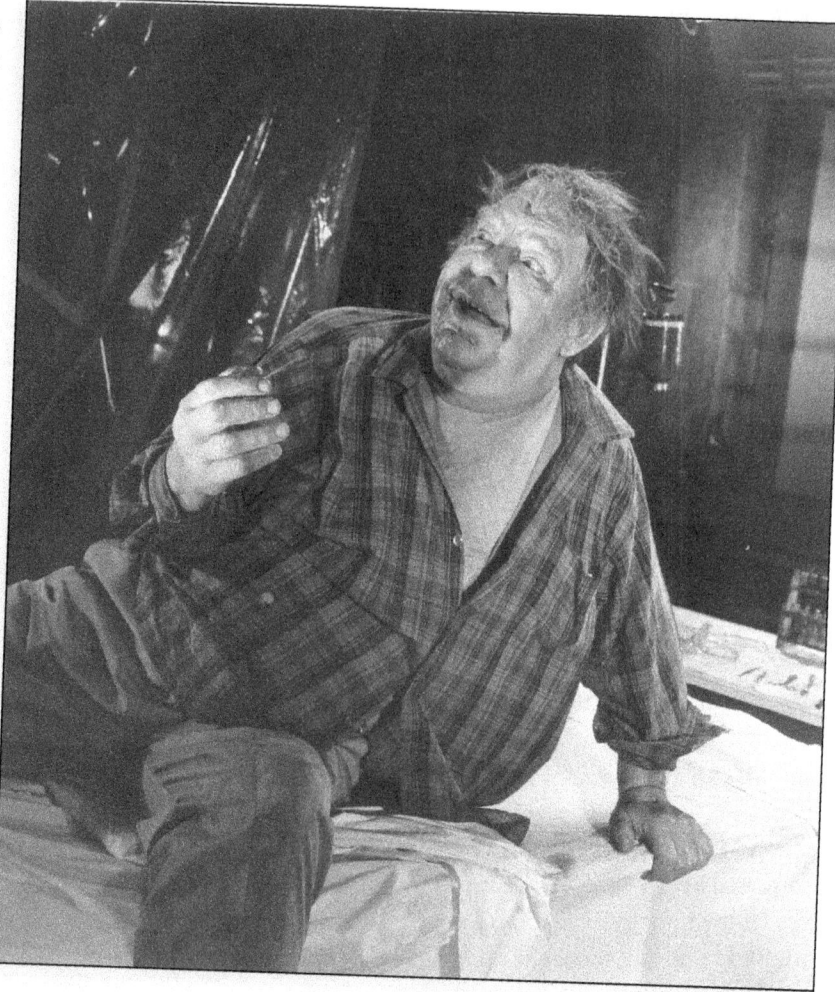

Like "Butcher" Benton, Chaney lost *his* voice (due to cancer, not a 287,000-volt charge). He withdrew from the Screen Actors Guild in November 1972; after a year in and out of hospitals for liver- and gout-related health woes, he died at his San Clemente home in July 1973 at age 67. His body was donated to a medical laboratory... presumably not one in the basement of an electrical power receiving station. (Photo above: Chaney in *Dracula vs. Frankenstein*.)

Shurlock said that the expression "God help us" should be delivered with reverence, and called for the elimination of the two *damn*s. (As a result, Lauder begins his on-screen tirade with "Blast it, man...") He also stressed that the PCA could not approve any of the typical strip numbers which are found in burlesque theaters; that dance movements such as bumps and grinds were unacceptable; and pointed out that even the life-sized cardboard cut-out of Eva, on display outside the theater, "must show her in a costume that avoids any undue exposure."

Interview with CASEY ADAMS

The *Indestructible Man* star dictates the wrap-up on the "Butcher" Benton package
By Tom Weaver

A native of Kansas, Casey Adams (real name: Max Showalter) picked up the acting bug as a toddler, when his mother used to bring him to the local theater where she played the piano for silent movies. He acted in 92 shows at the Pasadena Playhouse between 1935 and 1938, made his Broadway debut under the aegis of Oscar Hammerstein II in *Knights of Song* and acted for two years in the cast of Irving Berlin's traveling musical *This Is the Army*. In addition to his long list of films, TV appearances and stage shows, he was also a composer, songwriter and painter. When I interviewed him in 1996, he was living in an 18th century farmhouse in the Connecticut town he fell in love with while shooting the movie *It Happened to Jane* there in the summer of 1958.

My full interview with Adams, in which he talks about his early 1950s stint at 20th Century-Fox (and also *The Monster That Challenged the World*) appears in my McFarland book *Science Fiction and Fantasy Film Flashbacks*.

Tom Weaver: How did you become involved on Indestructible Man?
Casey Adams: I think Jack Pollexfen, who was the director and the p, called my agent and said that he wanted me to do it. Of course, that was a low-budget film, but I *loved* working with Lon Chaney! He was a pussycat, just a dear, dear man. He was *so* much like Broderick Crawford, who I'd done *Night People* with; Lon was *so* like Crawford. Also in the picture was a

Adams (right) and Stuart Randall in *Indestructible Man*. Adams' narration, combined with the use of practical locations, give parts of the movie a bit of the semi-documentary flavor of crime and spy movies of the 1940s—not to mention TV's *Dragnet*.

boy I'd been in *This Is the Army* with, Ross Elliott, and Marian Carr, who played the burlesque queen. I don't think she ever did another film after that [laughs]! She was trying *so* hard to be like Marilyn in a lot of the scenes—I wasn't conscious of that until I looked at the film on tape just the other day. I would *love* to have seen her on the burlesque stage, but I don't think they'd have *dared* to shoot *that* [laughs]!

The actor was born Max Showalter, and used that name on his later movies, including the favorites *10* (1979) and *Sixteen Candles* (1984). He seems to try hard to hit all the right notes as *Indestructible Man*'s dogged detective, but since movie fans are used to seeing him in light, often comic roles, he may not pull it off.

TW: What was it you liked about Chaney? What else can you recall about him?
Adams: Well, I could never keep up with him when we'd have a drink or two [*laughs*]! We'd go out to a restaurant or a bar, just the two of us, and he'd drink *me* under the table—I just couldn't keep up! It was just all very *pleasant*—I can't remember the exact conversations and all of that. He was a nice, considerate, thoughtful man and (I think) a very good actor.

TW: And Jack Pollexfen—what was he like?
Adams: It's very strange, I can't remember too much about Jack Pollexfen. A lot was just *shoved* at us and there was not much help [direction] in the scenes at all—he'd say, "You do what you feel is *right*." (A lot of times I *like* that.)

...Basically, *Indestructible Man* had a Frankenstein theme—bringing a man back to life. Oh, God, we shot in the Los Angeles sewer for *days*, and come the weekend I thought, "Oh, thank God!" And they *called* me Sunday night and said, "The film didn't come out. We've got to go back again into the sewer!" We had to go back and shoot it all over again! The smell—you can't *imagine* what it's like [*laughs*]! Oh, God! We did that film very quickly and we used all the locations in LA – they built practically nothing. The office was on a sound stage, but we went to a burlesque house downtown and shot stuff down there.

TW: That's one of the great things about it, all the location shooting on the streets of Los Angeles.
Adams: There were two locations used that were just incredible: One was Angels Flight, where the little railroad cars went up and down the hill. That's all gone, that's been torn down, but it was a wonderful, wonderful section. And then the building [the Bradbury building] used in the scene where Chaney goes into it to kill one man. That was a fantastic building with an exposed elevator and wrought iron railings and a glass ceiling. It's the kind of building that should always be saved by the historical people of Los Angeles, because it's a classic, classic building. And a fabulous "set" for us!

TW: Would you agree that those miserable scenes of you and Marian Carr in the parked car just go on forever?
Adams: Oh, my God! Oh! *Interminable*! And nothing happens! She tells the long story about her whole life and all of that...

TW: And then you jump in with the long story of *your* life!
Adams: It went on much too long! And that car had no windshield, you'll notice! I remember I told my sister, "I'm the leading man now in this film"—she was at Kansas University. Well, she couldn't *wait* until it opened, and when it did, she took a whole group of friends. And then she called me and she said, "*Why* did you tell me to see that film?? It was just *awful*." [*Laughs*] "We all *hated* it! It's the worst film you've ever done!"

TW: What did *you* think of it, seeing it again recently?
Adams: I didn't think it was as bad as I *thought* it was! It holds your interest, I think, and I wasn't embarrassed, as I thought I would be.

TW: Were you suited to play that Joe Friday like cop?
Adams: It was fun for me to *try*, because that's so far from *me*, that kind of thing. I was surprised they asked me, but I was tickled to death to do it, because it was another "character" kind of thing. And at least I got the girl [*laughs*]!

By Dr. Robert J. Kiss

[1] Early playdates

Indestructible Man opened as a supporting feature to *Invasion of the Body Snatchers* at selected theaters across the state of Illinois, including in the city of Chicago, between March 7 and March 10, 1956. Its premiere—*though not specifically billed as such*—was likely at the Freeport Theatre in Freeport, Illinois, where it was scheduled to start playing at 8:35 p.m., following a 7:10 p.m. screening of *Body Snatchers*.

From March 14, there followed a staggered nationwide general release of *Indestructible Man*, commencing in western and southwestern states, but already taking in theaters from coast to coast by the end of the month.

[2] As a standalone feature, March to September 1956

Within the sample of around 900 movie theaters across the U.S. during this period, approximately four percent of all screenings of *Indestructible Man* took the form of a standalone presentation supported only by "selected shorts." This form of presentation was attested solely in smaller towns where single bills were generally the norm anyway.

[3] Regular Allied Artists co-features, March to September 1956

[3.1] *Invasion of the Body Snatchers*

Within the sample of around 900 movie theaters across the U.S. during this period, 61 percent of all screenings of *Indestructible Man* were double-billed with *Invasion of the Body Snatchers*, meaning that this was both the movie's most regular co-feature, and the single most common way to see the movie during its first run. This double bill was attested during all months and in all states, and also received limited use as a Friday the 13th double bill on April 13. *Indestructible Man* was second-billed in all instances, without exception.

When *Body Snatchers* had initially opened in February 1956, its (arguably rather ill-matched) co-feature had been *Shack Out on 101*. During the first week of March, it started to be paired instead with *The Atomic Man* (aka *Timeslip*), but *Indestructible Man* soon replaced this as the movie's regular supporting feature on double bills from mid-March onwards.

[3.2] *World Without End*

From its opening in March, *Indestructible Man* was also regularly paired with *World Without End*, with 20 percent of all screenings of the movie within the sample taking the form of this double bill. *Indestructible Man* was once again second-billed in all instances, without exception. This double bill was evidenced primarily in locations where *Invasion of the Body Snatchers* had already played with either *Shack Out on 101* or *The Atomic Man* in support.

[3.3] *The Atomic Man*

Beginning in May, *Indestructible Man* also started

to be paired with *The Atomic Man*, with five percent of all screenings of the movie within the sample taking the form of this double bill. In roughly one-third of instances, *Indestructible Man* was top-billed, the only time this occurred during the movie's first run.

The "supporting feature" status of *Indestructible Man* led to the movie receiving extremely few reviews in contemporary newspapers, generally dismissed in a single sentence at the end of reviews of *Invasion of the Body Snatchers* or *World Without End*, that stated simply: "The co-feature is *Indestructible Man*, starring Lon Chaney." A somewhat extreme example can be found in Theresa Loeb Cone's May 16 review of *World Without End* in the *Oakland* (California) *Tribune*, which concludes: "*World Without End* is a very silly item indeed. Could be that the Fox bill gains from its co-feature, *Indestructible Man*. But, frankly, I didn't stay to see this Lon Chaney starrer."

[4] Other co-features, May to September 1956

In a lesser number of instances from May 1956 onwards, *Indestructible Man* played in support of a different feature to the three Allied Artists releases cited above. All of these other double-bill pairings collectively make up just ten percent of the total for first-run screenings of *Indestructible Man* within the sample, and were attested primarily at lower-rung small-town and neighborhood theaters.

These other features are arranged alphabetically below; the month mentioned in each case is the earliest in which I've found the pairing attested among the sample of around 900 movie theaters across the U.S. In all instances, *Indestructible Man* was the second feature on the bill.

August 1956	*Battle Cry* (Warner Brothers; Van Heflin)
August 1956	*The Big Sky* (RKO; Kirk Douglas)
June 1956	*The Broken Star* (United Artists; Howard Duff)
August 1956	*Crashing Las Vegas* (Allied Artists; The Bowery Boys)
July 1956	*Foreign Intrigue* (United Artists; Robert Mitchum)
May 1956	*Hell's Horizon* (Columbia; Marla English)
September 1956	*Johnny Concho* (United Artists; Frank Sinatra)
May 1956	*The Man Who Never Was* (20th Century-Fox; Clifton Webb)
July 1956	*Ransom!* (MGM; Glenn Ford)
August 1956	*Safari* (Columbia; Victor Mature)
August 1956	*Satellite in the Sky* (Warner Brothers; Lois Maxwell); *Satellite* and *Indestructible* were paired for a substantial number of playdates.
September 1956	*The Searchers* (Warner Brothers; John Wayne)

[5] Triple and quadruple bills, September 1956

Indestructible Man started to appear on triple and quadruple bills at drive-ins only during the final week of September 1956, and exclusively as a return appearance in locations where its first run had already taken place. These initial multiple-bill screenings thus fall outside the remit of the movie's first-run history, and are of note only insofar as they continued to include one of the movie's regular Allied Artists co-features, in the form of either *Invasion of the Body Snatchers* or *World Without End*.

The Man from Planet X Goes Looney Tunes

By Tom Weaver

Jack Pollexfen and Aubrey Wisberg—flying saucer coverer-uppers?? We find that implication in the 1997 bestseller *The Day Before Roswell* by Col. Philip J. Corso, who after decades of military service wrote that book in which he claimed to have stewarded the Roswell alien artifacts. "Flying saucers did truly buzz over Washington, D.C., in 1952," Corso insisted,

and there are plenty of photographs and radar reports to substantiate it. But we [the government and military] denied it while encouraging science fiction writers to make movies like *The Man from Planet X* to blow off some of the pressure concerning the truth about flying disks. This was called camouflage through limited disclosure, and it worked. If people could enjoy it as entertainment, get duly frightened, and follow trails to nowhere that the working group had planted, then they'd be less likely to stumble over what we were really doing.

As Robert Guffey wrote in his as-yet-unpublished article "*The Man from Planet X*—Hollywood's First Invasion from Outer Space," if either Pollexfen or Wisberg "operated as a witting tool of Col. Corso's military team," as Corso suggests, they took that secret to their graves with them.

Pollexfen's first sci-fi character, the Man from Planet X (played by five-foot actor Pat Goldin, pictured on right) was the advance scout for a mass migration to Earth. He didn't quite pull *that* off, but he did make a screen comeback a half-century later as one of the monster characters in the Area 52 scenes of director Joe Dante's *Looney Tunes: Back in Action* (2003). In the behind-the-scenes *Looney Tunes* shot below, X (played by John Munro Cameron) is flanked by mechanical designer-puppeteer Dave Penikas and puppeteer Garth Winkless; in the shot on the right, he's stored in a giant Mason jar.

Recommended Additional Viewing

Indestructible Man's confluence of gangsters and life-restoring scientists probably struck some 1956 moviegoers as unique. But the fact is that it was part of a proud sci-fi film tradition with its roots back in the 1930s "Golden Age"—most memorably Boris Karloff's *The Walking Dead* (1936). Vintage chillers where killers and/or criminals get a second shot at life, either in their own bodies or someone else's, include *Supernatural* (1933), *The Return of Doctor X* (1939), *Black Friday* (1940), *The Man with Two Lives* (1942), *Bowery at Midnight* (1942), *The Lady and the Monster* (1944) and *The Phantom Speaks* (1945); then there are the serials *Dick Tracy's G-Men* (1939), *Gang Busters* (1942) and *Captain America* (1944).* Karloff bounces back again in *The Man They Could Not Hang* (1939); in one of the best of the bunch, *The Monster and the Girl* (1941), a man executed for a murder he didn't commit subsequently has his brain transplanted into the body of an ape, and settles scores with a group of gangsters.

Three back-from-the-dead movies you probably haven't seen are reviewed below:

6 Hours to Live (Fox, 1932) Warner Baxter, Miriam Jordan, John Boles, George F. Marion Sr. Directed by William Dieterle.

This genre gem segues story-wise from political drama to romance to murder mystery to sci-fi, and then to religious-inspirational artfully flavored with the macabre. In Geneva, diplomat Warner Baxter, representing the republic of Sylvaria, has upset the world's economic apple cart by being the one "no" vote at an ongoing international trade conference. He's doing it for the most admirable patriotic reasons but is now a hated man; on the eve of the final ballot, in the bedroom of the estate where he's staying, he's strangled by a mystery intruder. But another guest, scientist George Marion Sr., has developed a Kenneth Strickfaden-ish ray machine that can revive the dead for six hours. Baxter comes back looking like his old self but, like Karloff in *The Walking Dead*, omniscient about all things on *both* sides of the veil. There's even a touch of *Indestructible Man* when it turns out that the ray has not only resurrected him but apparently made him un-killable: Baxter casually walks away from a high-speed car crash. And, like other movie characters

"Recently Fox has been trying stories that are off the beaten path," wrote *Variety* reviewer Char. "*Six Hours to Live* tackles its idea in a somewhat fantastic manner, instilling a certain interest even if [the movie] will leave audiences thinking it nutty."

---

* In *Captain America*, the Scarab's (Lionel Atwill) henchman Matson (George J. Lewis) is killed in a fall but later revived by a scientist's life-restoring machine. The Scarab tells him, "You should be thankful, Matson. You're the only authentic case **in modern times** of a man who has returned from the dead." It isn't every serial that gives a between-the-lines shout-out to Jesus Christ and the Resurrection!

The stars of *Decoy* (1946): On the left, Edward Norris, who died in 1942 in *The Man with Two Lives* and was brought back to life by a doctor; on the right, Herbert Rudley, who died in 1956 in *The Black Sleep* and was brought back to life by a surgeon; and in the middle, 30-year-old Jean Gillie, who died in 1949…period

who have embarked on round trips to the beyond, Baxter doesn't think much of the idea and makes it one of his final orders of business to destroy Marion's machine and give the scientist a good tongue-lashing.

One favorite moment: Talking about Marion's deaf-mute assistant Dewey Robinson, Baxter (knowing all there is to know about the Afterlife) says, "Would you tell him some time for me, professor, that he won't be deaf and dumb *always*."

Decoy (Monogram, 1946) Jean Gillie, Edward Norris, Robert Armstrong, Herbert Rudley. Directed by Jack Bernhard.

Prior to the start of this movie, Robert Armstrong, murderous bank truck robber, was caught and sentenced to die. After his gas chamber execution, his body is stolen and he's brought back from the dead; for Armstrong, that's the good news. The *bad* news is that Dr. Herbert Rudley has resuscitated him at the behest of his (Armstrong's) cash-mad moll Jean Gillie and crook Edward Norris, who couldn't care less about Armstrong's vital signs (or lack thereof), just the fact that he died without revealing the hiding place of 400 grand in bank loot. Once Armstrong draws a map, Norris draws a bead; Armstrong dies for the second time in one night, this time for keeps. Now that the movie's borderline sci-fi angle is gone with a puff of gunsmoke, its story meanders into thieves-fall-out territory, with Gillie dishing up proof positive that the female of the species is deadlier than the male. In real life, the English actress was the wife of *Decoy*'s writer-director Jack Bernhard and the movie was a vehicle for her, including a cameo in the opening credits ("Introducing Miss JEAN GILLIE"). By the time *Decoy* was released, Bernhard and Gillie had split. Gillie died at her London home just three years later, at 33.

As proof that all roads lead to Lon Chaney Jr., Bernhard was the associate producer of *Man Made Monster*, another movie with a man (Chaney) living after the boys in the prison death house had done their darnedest; and *Decoy* life-restorer Rudley is the "dead" convict who *gets* revived in *The Black Sleep* (1956), *also* with Chaney. And while we're at it, Edward Norris played the title character in *The Man with Two Lives*, Robert Armstrong co-starred in *Gang Busters* and *Decoy* screenwriter Ned Young acted in 1943's *Dead Men Walk!* The New York Times' Thomas M. Pryor wrote, "Maybe [*Decoy*'s screenwriters] thought they had done something startling by having a doctor restore the heartbeat of a convict who had just been carried out of State gas chamber. But shucks, Karloff has done that time and again." Ten points to Pryor for remembering and mentioning that!

Harrison's Reports: "[T]he picture stands in a class by itself as a lesson in varied types of murders."

The Gas House Kids in Hollywood (PRC, 1947) Carl "Alfalfa" Switzer, Benny Bartlett, Rudy Wissler, Tommy Bond, James Burke. Directed by Edward L. Cahn.

Welllll, this isn't a back-from-the-dead movie, but semi-sorta-in-a-way, and I'm going to use that as an excuse to write about it. The "mad scientist" is Milton Parsons; instead of the sepulchral, creepy characters he often played, here he's actually a friendly, accommodating sort (and the father of pretty Jan Bryant). But mad nonetheless: In the basement laboratory of his secluded, museum-like Hollywood-area home, he is using the body of a recently deceased colleague as a link between our world and the next, hoping to access ancient sound waves and hear the speeches of long-dead historic figures. An East Side

Kids-like gaggle of New York teens, "The Gas House Kids" (Carl "Alfalfa" Switzer, Benny Bartlett, Rudy Wissler, Tommy Bond), have driven cross-country to meet their favorite Hollywood star (Michael Whalen) and are staying with the professor; when dead bodies start appearing and disappearing in the house, the kids want to scram but a doofus police lieutenant (James Burke) makes them stay. Strange noises are ascribed to the ghost of the prospector who supposedly haunts the house but, *à la Hold That Ghost* (1941) and probably 20 other movies, the culprits are crooks trying to scare away the house's inhabitants as they (the crooks) search in secret passageways for the prospector's fortune. In one surprising scene, "Alfalfa" falls into a swimming pool and two of his friends dive in to save him; one pulls up "Alfalfa" by his hair, the other pulls up the corpse of a murdered man whose body was hidden in the pool! Parsons' lab may be the worst seen in *any* of these movies, nothing but a few flashing lights (etc.) and a table far too short for the body of his late colleague, whose legs extend out into space way past the table's edge. This was the third and last Gas House Kids movie, after *Gas House Kids* (1946) and *Gas House Kids Go West* (1947), and being a PRC it definitely should have been included in my 1993 McFarland book *Poverty Row Horrors!* but I forgot all about it. The most fantastic part of it isn't using a corpse as a conduit to a world of dead men's voices, but that the Gas House Kids' favorite movie star is…*Michael Whalen*?!?

This sordid and violent film noir from first-time director Jack Bernhard could have served as a template for the early scenes of *Indestructible Man*.

Indestructible Inspiration?

By Tom Weaver

Jack Pollexfen was raised in Mill Valley, California, and, after the end of his motion picture career, lived out the rest of his life there. A nut for history, he soaked up a lot of local lore. Is it possible that, some time before the production of *Indestructible Man*, Pollexfen read *The San Quentin Story*, the 1950 autobiography of the prison's warden Clinton T. Duffy? Check out Duffy's account of a strange incident involving Condemned Row inmate Thomas McMonigle, gas chamber-bound for killing a 15-year-old high school girl…and consider the possibility that it might have provided some *Indestructible* inspiration:

"After I'm dead," [McMonigle] said, peering at me with his frosty blue eyes, "my body belongs to me or whoever claims it. Ain't that so?"

"I suppose it is."

"And if a guy wants to bring me back to life, that's okay too, huh?"

I looked at him closely, but there wasn't a flicker on his broad face. I had seen other men lose their minds on the Row when the clock began to cut them down…

"You feel all right, Mac?" I asked.

"Why, sure, Warden. You prob'ly think I'm kiddin', but I ain't. I know a guy who can do it. He's got a machine that'll bring me out of it after I get the gas."

"All right, all right," I said soothingly. I was sure now that his mind was at least temporarily unbalanced and that a psychiatric examination was in order. I told McMonigle I'd think it over and let him know. The following morning I was visited by Dr. Robert Cornish[*], a Berkeley scientist who had achieved considerable notoriety some years before with an involved method of bringing dogs back to life after he killed them in his laboratory. Dr. Cornish frankly admitted that he had a similar plan for reviving McMonigle after the execution and was convinced it would be as successful as it had been with the dogs.

I was so intrigued by his proposal that I played along with it for quite a while, but soon realized that he and McMonigle were serious and fully intended to carry out the experiment. Dr. Cornish wanted to take McMonigle's body from the gas chamber as soon as the prison physician pronounced him dead. He planned to inject antidotes, stimulants, and other fluids directly into the veins, and to place McMonigle's body into a machine that would set the blood in motion and eventually induce a heartbeat.

"Doctor," I said, "can't you find a subject somewhere else, maybe a carbon monoxide victim?"

"I've tried half a dozen times," he said, "but I can never get to them soon enough. I must have the body immediately."

I told him he would have exactly the same problem in the gas chamber, because McMonigle's body would have to remain there at least an hour. The concentration of hydrocyanic gas in that small space is so dense, and so terribly dangerous, that powerful blowers are kept running for half an hour to pump it out, and at

---

[*]Every Monster Kid knows that Dr. Cornish's experiments with dogs inspired the dreadful movie *Life Returns*, made in 1934, featuring Cornish in a supporting role, and incorporating footage of one of his canine "resurrections."

the same time the chamber and its apparatus are neutralized with ammonia. There is another half-hour safety period after that, and even then the men who remove the prisoner's body wear gas masks and rubber gloves. "The only way you can do this," I said a little impatiently, "is for you to sit alongside McMonigle in the other [gas chamber] chair, so you'll be handy."

"Maybe I will do that," he snapped.

Dr. Cornish went away in a huff, and I thought that would put an end to this grim fantasy. But when the courts denied McMonigle's appeal and set the execution for February 20, 1948, Dr. Cornish called at my office twice more, demanding a chance to try his invention. I had to tell him quite bluntly that I wouldn't discuss it again without orders from some higher authority.

Newspapers had covered this macabre saga right from the beginning. On March 13, 1947, the *Oakland Tribune* published on its front page a reproduction of McMonigle's handwritten letter to Cornish; alongside it, the article "Savant May Cheat Death" stated that Cornish was fully aware that his plan "might ring of alchemy to state officials and perhaps in some of the public." The biochemist claimed that similar experiments had been conducted in other countries "and with reported success in Russia." The article continued:

> Dr. Cornish, who dropped his experiments along these lines 13 years ago after the governors of various states rejected his appeal for the body of an executed convict, sent a new request to Gov. Earl Warren after talking with McMonigle in San Quentin's death row.
>
> …If permission is granted, Dr. Cornish said he would need at least six months to complete arrangements for the experiment.
>
> He would probably use the technique developed by Dr. Alexis Carrel and Charles Lindbergh on keeping organs alive, he said, and would have the added advantages of blood plasma and the assistance of a trained surgeon.
>
> Before conducting the test on McMonigle, Dr. Cornish said he would experiment again with dogs until convinced he could completely defeat the tenacious grip of death on an animal.

In a United Press story published at this same time, Cornish said that McMonigle wanted to be brought back to life "in the interest of science. He makes the offer, he told me, in interests of thousands who died of shock, asphyxiation and drowning."

Cornish made the papers again in June by saying he'd kill a sheep and bring it back to life to prove he could resuscitate the convicted sex slayer. This UP story continued,

> Cornish, 43, said he would kill the sheep in a gas chamber next week under conditions simulating the San Quentin gas chamber. The sheep will be killed with cyanide gas in a miniature reproduction of California's lethal gas chamber.
>
> Cornish will attempt to revive it in the same manner he successfully revived five dogs more than a decade ago.
>
> The sheep's jugular vein will be slit, Cornish said, and oxygen pumped into the body to replace the cyanide in the blood stream.
>
> …The scientist admitted McMonigle's nervous system might be affected seriously by the shock of death and a return to life—but no more than a victim of prolonged carbon monoxide poisoning or even severe measles.

On February 15, 1948, Cornish dramatically demonstrated an artificial heart and lung in a shed behind his tooth powder factory at 743 Dwight Way in Berkeley and announced that he was preparing a letter to Governor Warren asking for a 60-day stay of execution for McMonigle.

Ultimately, no resurrection was attempted.

The night before he paid the ultimate penalty for his crime, McMonigle ate a chicken dinner and smoked many cigars; the next morning, his breakfast order was ham and eggs. Eggs weren't the only thing that cracked that morning; according to Warden Duffy, McMonigle entered the gas chamber "sobbing and hopefully searching the audience for a familiar face." Soon he quieted down, and sat stoically as the white cyanide pellets dropped into a bucket beneath the death chamber chair. Convicted despite the absence of a *corpus delicti*, McMonigle took to the grave the secret of where he disposed of the body of the bobby soxer.

McMonigle was not the first gas chamber casualty who had a doctor in his rooting section, anxious to restore him to life; that goes back to *the very beginning*, at least in the U.S. The first person ever to be executed via lethal gas in America was immigrant Gee Jon, who sat down in the Nevada State Prison death chamber's unpainted pine chair and drew his last breath in 1924. This being a new procedure, there was great trepidation regarding the safe removal of the body from the gas chamber, but finally it was delivered to the prison hospital where the doctors were in no hurry to get too close. The medicos were almost unanimous in agreeing that he was dead: The one hold-out, a Dr. Turner, insisted that the gentleman "was still alive enough to be resuscitated and he wanted to inject the body with camphor to bring him back to life, 'in the interests of science.'" (Dr. Turner—and Dr. Cornish—both seem to miss the point of an execution!) Scott Christianson's book *The Last Gasp: The Rise and Fall of the American Gas Chamber*, the source of the preceding quote, goes on:

> Turner also claimed that when Gee's body was removed from the death cell two and a half hours after his execution, it was still warm and lacking any signs of rigor mortis, which led him to believe it would have been possible to resuscitate Gee using a little electric shock, some warm blankets, and a pulmonator. Turner later startled an audience at the Reno Lions Club by suggesting that Gee probably "died of cold and exposure." He also suggested…that all bodies removed from gas chambers in the future should be shot or hanged to ensure they were dead.

Indestructible Man's opening scene of Paul Lowe visiting the Butcher is presumably set on San Quentin's Condemned Row, which in real life is where Benton would *be* the day before his execution. To get an idea what it was like for Benton to walk the last mile, catch director Robert Wise's *I Want to Live!* (1958), the story of prostitute-crook Barbara Graham's (Oscar winner Susan Hayward) murder conviction and her 1955 gas chamber execution. That movie's San Quentin gas chamber set, and the procedure, are said to be authentic down to the last detail. In your mind, just superimpose Lon Chaney over Susan Hayward.

AD SECTION

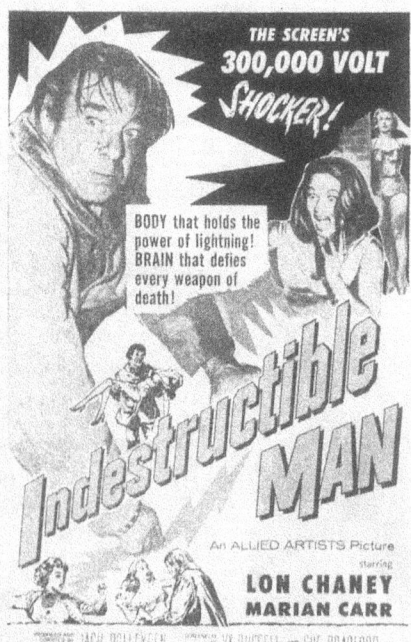

POSTERS and LOBBY DISPLAYS

THREE SHEET

The full line of **Posters** and **Lobbies** is available through National Screen Service Exchanges

ONE SHEET

Set of Eight Full Color
11 x 14 Lobby Photos
Also Available

TWO 22 x 28 LOBBY CARDS

37 Allied Artists Exchanges to Serve You

Albany, N. Y.	New Orleans, Louisiana
Atlanta, Georgia	New York, New York
Boston, Massachusetts	Oklahoma City, Oklahoma
Buffalo, New York	Omaha, Nebraska
Cincinnati, Ohio	Philadelphia, Pennsylvania
Charlotte, North Carolina	Pittsburgh, Pennsylvania
Chicago, Illinois	Portland, Oregon
Cleveland, Ohio	St. Louis, Missouri
Dallas, Texas	Salt Lake City, Utah
Denver, Colorado	San Francisco, California
Des Moines, Iowa	Seattle, Washington
Detroit, Michigan	Washington, D. C.
Indianapolis, Indiana	Toronto, Ontario
Kansas City, Missouri	Montreal, Quebec
Los Angeles, California	Winnipeg, Manitoba
Memphis, Tennessee	St. John, N. B.
Milwaukee, Wisconsin	Calgary, Alberta
Minneapolis, Minnesota	Vancouver, B. C.
New Haven, Connecticut	

ALLIED ARTISTS PICTURES CORP.
4376 Sunset Drive, Hollywood 27, California
and
1560 Broadway, New York, N. Y.

INSERT CARD

COMPLETE CAMPAIGN MAT 35¢

ALL THE AD AND SCENE CUTS BELOW AVAILABLE ON ONE BIG BARGAIN MAT!

ORDER "INDESTRUCTIBLE MAN" SPECIAL MAT NO. 1 FROM NATIONAL SCREEN

NOTE: Any of These Mats May Be Ordered Singly at the Regular Price. Order by Number Under the Cut.

★ PUBLICITY ★

MAN IMPERVIOUS TO BULLETS TERRIFIES IN MURDER SIEGE

Lon Chaney creates a superman who is impervious to bullets and all other manner of missiles in "Indestructible Man," a screen chiller from Allied Artists, now showing at the .... theatre.

To get the proper effect as police hand-guns and rifles sprayed shots at him point blank, Chaney wore a bullet-proof vest, and although the cartridges in the weapons were blank, the blasts knocked him off of his feet several times, and his outer clothing was nearly burned.

A great deal of the action of the picture takes place in the 700-mile underground storm drainage system of Los Angeles, a sprawling giant spider web of vast tunnels large enough to swallow army tanks.

Through this labyrinth Chaney is pursued by a small army of law enforcement officers, some of them carrying acid tanks, flame throwers in the relentless hunt for the mad killer.

Featured supporting roles in the picture are played by Casey Adams as a detective in charge of the hunt, Marian Carr as a burlesque dancer and friend of Chaney's before he became a killer, Ross Elliott as a crooked lawyer and Stuart Randall as a police captain.

The picture was produced and directed by Jack Pollexfen from an original screenplay by Sue Bradford and Vy Russell.

Under-City Maze Is Police Trap

One of the engineering wonders of the world, the 700-mile storm drain system of the city of Los Angeles, with many tunnels large enough to swallow a freight train, is the maze in which police finally entrap Lon Chaney, portraying a homicidal maniac, in "Indestructible Man," an Allied Artists screen chiller, now at the .... theatre.

Chaney, in a role reminiscent of those made famous by his father, portrays a convict executed for murder who is brought back to life by a mad scientist, and who in his next life phase cannot be killed by modern methods.

Casey Adams, Marian Carr, Stuart Randall and Ross Elliott have featured roles in the picture, which was produced and directed by Jack Pollexfen.

Cast

The Butcher	LON CHANEY
Chasen	CASEY ADAMS
Eva Martin	MARIAN CARR
Paul Lowe	ROSS ELLIOTT
Police Captain	STUART RANDALL
Joe Marcellini	KEN TERRELL
Squeamy Ellis	MARVIN ELLIS
Prof. Bradshaw	ROBERT SHAYNE

Synopsis
(Not for Publication)

The Butcher (Lon Chaney) goes to his death in the gas chamber at San Quentin, cursing three men who had crossed him: Squeamy Ellis (Marvin Ellis), Joe Marcellini (Ken Terrell) and Paul Lowe (Ross Elliott), his attorney. He dies without revealing the hiding place of $600,000, stolen in an armored car holdup. A Los Angeles detective, Chasen (Casey Adams), watches The Butcher's former associates, particularly Eva Martin (Marian Carr), a burlesque dancer. The Butcher's body is stolen by Professor Bradshaw (Robert Shayne) and restored to life in the form of an Indestructible Man. In this form, leaving a trail of dead in his wake, The Butcher returns to Los Angeles and kills Squeamy and Marcellini. Lowe, the attorney, learns of The Butcher's return and tips off the police. The Butcher seeks the haven of the vast Los Angeles storm drain system and ends up in a power station where he destroys himself with a super electrical charge.

Chaney Due In Chiller Role
(Advance)

Lon Chaney, famed creator of fantastic screen characters as his father was before him, plays the title role in "Indestructible Man," a screen thriller from Allied Artists which will open at the .... theatre next ....

As a man executed for murder and then brought back to life by a mad scientist, Chaney is impervious to flame throwers, bullets and all other forms of weapons as he flees from the police through the mazes of the 700-mile Los Angeles storm drain system.

Casey Adams, Marian Carr, Ross Elliott and Stuart Randall have featured roles in the Jack Pollexfen production.

Bullets Bounce From Iron Man

A screen writer's conception of a man who cannot be killed by bullets, flame throwers or any other form of modern weapons, is portrayed by Lon Chaney in "Indestructible Man," a screen thriller from Allied Artists, currently showing at the .... theatre.

Chaney's role is that of a convicted murderer, brought back to life after his execution in the San Quentin gas chamber by a mad scientist who bribes a mortician to get the body. It is in this new life phase that Chaney literally becomes indestructible.

Casey Adams, Marian Carr, Ross Elliott and Stuart Randall head the featured cast. Jack Pollexfen produced and directed.

Funicular Used To Build Drama

One of the few funicular railways remaining in public use in the United States, the 81-year-old Angel's Flight rising from Los Angeles' original business section to once-fashionable Bunker Hill, now a blighted area, is a unique setting used for one of the most dramatic sequences of "Indestructible Man," starring Lon Chaney, now at the .... theatre.

In featured roles are Casey Adams, Marian Carr, Stuart Randall and Ross Elliott, with Chaney portraying a man brought back to life after being executed for murder, and who cannot again be killed in his new life phase.

The picture was produced and directed for Allied Artists by Jack Pollexfen.

Credits

Produced and Directed by Jack Pollexfen. Original Screenplay by Sue Bradford and Vy Russell. Music by Albert Glasser. Film Editor Fred Feitshans Jr., A.C.E. Photographed by John Russell Jr., A.S.C. Art Director Ted Holsopple. Production Manager Chris Beute.

Murder Trail Is Left By Chaney

A gruesome trail of murders for revenge is left by Lon Chaney as a man impervious to gun fire, flame throwers and all other manner of weapons in "Indestructible Man," a screen thriller now showing at the .... theatre.

Chaney portrays a man executed for murder in the gas chamber at San Quentin who is brought back to life in the laboratory of a mad scientist. In his new life phase Chaney cannot be killed again by any known methods, and he sets off on his path of revenge slayings.

Marian Carr, Casey Adams, Ross Elliott and Stuart Randall have featured roles in the film, produced and directed for Allied Artists by Jack Pollexfen.

BACK STAGE PLEA

Lon Chaney appeals for help from his former girl friend, Marian Carr, back stage in a burlesque theatre in Allied Artists' shock film "Indestructible Man," currently showing at the .... theatre.

LON CHANEY CARRIES ON IN TRADITION OF FAMOUS DAD

The second generation Lon Chaney is carrying on in the tradition of his screen star father, famous in the days of silent pictures and in the early years of sound as a wizard of makeup, whose role as the hunchback dwarf in the original production of "The Phantom of the Opera," remains one of the most memorable characterizations ever given on the screen.

The present-day Lon Chaney is also a specialist in eerie makeup, having a theatrical dressing room in his North Hollywood house where he experiments with various effects, and where he worked out the startling disguise he uses in "Indestructible Man," the chiller now at the .... theatre.

Chaney had to get the effect of a human face after it has been seared by the inferno blast from a flame thrower, a weapon employed by the police who are chasing him after they become aware that bullets, even from high powered rifles, merely bounce from his skin. Even the flame thrower doesn't stop him as a man follows his murderous path.

Heading the featured supporting cast are Casey Adams as a detective, Marian Carr as a burlesque  dancer, Ross Elliott as a crooked attorney and Stuart Randall as a captain of police.

The picture was produced and directed for Allied Artists by Jack Pollexfen.

Marian Carr Is Burlesque Girl

Marian Carr, famed as a magazine cover girl and photographers' model before she went to Hollywood, had to add to her many talents for her role with Lon Chaney in Allied Artists' screen chiller, "Indestructible Man," currently at the .... theatre.

To prepare for her role as a burlesque dancer, Marian spent several hours a day backstage at one of Los Angeles' Main Street burlesque houses, taking lessons from the strippers, the grinders and the bumpers, and from the regular girls in the line.

As the "Indestructible Man," Chaney, the object of a manhunt in the maze of the 700-mile Los Angeles storm drain system, is impervious to bullets, flame throwers, and all other types of weapons.

With Miss Carr are Casey Adams, Ross Elliott and Stuart Randall in top featured roles. Jack Pollexfen produced and directed.

DANCER

Lovely Marian Carr plays a burlesque dancer in "Indestructible Man," starring Lon Chaney as a mad killer. The Allied Artists thrill-film is currently showing at the .... theatre.

Electric Jungle Chase Setting

The main southern California terminal of the power lines that carry 7 million volts of electrical power from the Boulder Canyon dam to Los Angeles is but one of the many dramatic settings used for Allied Artists' screen chiller, "Indestructible Man," starring Lon Chaney, and now playing at the .... theatre.

This terrifying electrical jungle is where Chaney finally meets his death after a police chase through miles of the eerie tunnels of the Los Angeles municipal storm drain system.

Casey Adams, Marian Carr, Ross Elliott and Stuart Randall have featured roles in the picture which was produced and directed by Jack Pollexfen.

STALKED

Lon Chaney, in the title role, stalks Stewart Randall, a cop, in Allied Artists' shocker, "Indestructible Man," now at the .... theatre.

★ PUBLICITY ★

INDESTRUCTIBLE MAN

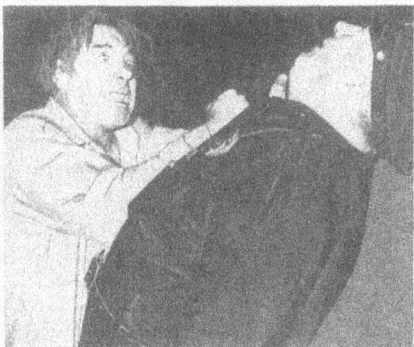

INDESTRUCTIBLE MAN No. 21

Lon Chaney portrays a super-man impervious to bullets, tear gas bombs and even flame throwers in Allied Artists' sensational "Indestructible Man," the current shock film at the .... theatre. Here he defies the law.

Casey Adams In Detective Role

Casey Adams, specialist in portraying parboiled lawmen and private detectives, joins the Los Angeles police force to track down Lon Chaney as a maniacal murderer in "Indestructible Man," a screen chiller from Allied Artists, currently at the .... theatre.

As a detective-lieutenant Adams directs a giant manhunt through the tunnel mazes of the city's fabulous 700-mile storm drainage system, one of the most dramatic settings ever devised for a film of its sort.

As the "Indestructible Man," Chaney, executed for murder and brought back to life by a mad scientist, is impervious to bullets, flame throwers, and all other manner of weapons until he destroys himself in the 7 million volt maze of a giant power plant.

The picture, produced and directed by Jack Pollexfen, features Marian Carr, Ross Elliott and Stuart Randall.

INDESTRUCTIBLE

Lon Chaney portrays a murderer who cannot be destroyed by guns, knives or flame throwers in Allied Artists' spine-tingling "Indestructible Man," now at the .... theatre, with Marian Carr and Casey Adams heading the supporting cast.

VAST STORM DRAIN SYSTEM SETTING FOR EERIE PICTURE
(Review)

A man-hunt through the cavernous tunnels of the Los Angeles storm drain system, a vast network totaling more than 700 miles in length, hits with a powerful dramatic punch as the eerie climax of "Indestructible Man," the screen thriller that opened yesterday at the .... theatre.

Starred in the title role is Lon Chaney, master of weird makeup as his father was before him, playing the role of a convicted murderer, executed in the gas chamber at San Quentin prison, but brought back to life in a daring laboratory experiment by a scientist who had secured Chaney's body by a bribe.

In his new form Chaney, impervious to bullets and with the strength of a locomotive, sets out on a trail of murder and revenge, but eventually meets death again in a climax that left yesterday's audience breathless.

Directing the hunt for the man that modern weapons cannot kill is Casey Adams as a detective captain, giving an excellent performance as a relentless law officer. He is helped in his search by Marian Carr as a shapely burlesque dancer who had been Chaney's girl friend in days past.

The picture was produced and directed for Allied Artists by Jack Pollexfen.

ESCAPE

INDESTRUCTIBLE MAN No. 2

Lon Chaney seeks refuge in the storm drain system in Allied Artists' sensational shock drama, "Indestructible Man," now at the .... theatre.

EERIE SETTING

The vast storm drain system of Los Angeles is the eerie underground setting for a wild chase in "Indestructible Man," an Allied Artists' chiller, now at the .... theatre.

THRILLER

"Indestructible Man," starring Lon Chaney as a revenge-killer who himself cannot be destroyed is the current thriller-hit at the .... theatre. Others in the Allied Artists production are Marian Carr and Casey Adams.

★ EXPLOITATION ★

Give Three Sheet Cutout Eerie Effect With Trick Lighting And Electrical Buzzer

The three sheet on "Indestructible Man" lends itself perfectly to a lobby or theatre front set-piece that is certain to catch the eye and ear of any passer-by. Mount the three sheet on beaver board and cutout as shown in the illustration on the right. Also cutout the single white lightning type streak that runs between the two jagged edge lines. On the back of the cutout, behind the line, paste strips of yellow gelatin so that when you spot lights in back of it, the strip will have a neon tube effect. In addition, have your electrician rig up a buzzer that will further enhance the value of the cutout.

Newspaper Overprint

The sensational idea of a maniacal killer brought back to life after being legally executed in a prison gas chamber suggests the use of a red-lettered newspaper overprint. Make arrangements to have your local paper run an extra supply (sufficient to fill your needs) of one day's issue for the purpose of overprinting. Use red ink for the overprint, with copy similar to this: MAD KILLER LIVES AFTER GAS CHAMBER EXECUTION . . . SEE "INDESTRUCTIBLE MAN!"

Contest Ideas

Here are three ideas for newspaper contests. Award guest tickets as prizes. Ask contestants to fill in title and submit a letter of 100 words or less on the following:
1) .... is the title of the horror story I enjoyed most because
2) .... is the title of the horror film I liked best because
3) .... is the title of the scariest picture in which Lon Chaney, Sr. (father of the star of "Indestructible Man") was starred and which I liked best because

SENSATIONALIZE LOBBY AND FRONT

"Indestructible Man" is an exploitation picture, sensational in theme, and should be handled as such. It's the ideal picture for a false front. The key art, contained in the three sheet cutout shown on this page, is pictured on all accessories available at NSS. These accessories, surrounded by a liberal display of action stills, will make up a front that should hypo your take at the boxoffice. Also check the suggestion of making up the special lobby piece as described elsewhere on this page.

Warning Notices

A different type of herald, in the form of an open letter to the people of your community, is particularly adaptable for exploitation purposes for "Indestructible Man." Similar copy can be used for window cards or for advance teaser ads. If you use heralds, display a two column ad on the bottom and add theatre name and playdate.

WARNING
TO THE PEOPLE OF BLANKTOWN!

A maniacal killer known as the Butcher, and recently executed at the state prison, is believed to be ALIVE AGAIN AND ON THE LOOSE! The authorities are certain that a mad doctor, known to them, came into possession of the body directly after the execution and restored the killer to life!

Keep your doors bolted and your windows locked at night and report anything of a suspicious nature to the police!

"HORROR" ANGLES

"Indestructible Man" contains a number of scary sequences guaranteed to satisfy that segment of the population who go for "horror" pictures. Tie in with horror mags and books. Darken house when showing the advance trailer. See if you get a local radio or TV MC to run a "Scream Contest," offering a small cash prize to the women giving out with the scariest scream. For your lobby and front select the stills with the type of action appealing to "horror" fans.

www.ingramcontent.com/pod-product-compliance
Lightning Source LLC
Chambersburg PA
CBHW080544170426
43195CB00016B/2681